BRIGHT LIGHTS

DARK PLACES

PASTOR
JIM,
THANK YOU FOR
YOUR HEART FOR
VEGAS! ENJOY THE
JOURNEY!
BLESS YOU

BRIGHT LIGHTS

DARK PLACES

Pioneering as a Female
Police Officer in Las Vegas

DEBRA GAUTHIER

TATE PUBLISHING & Enterprises

Published by Tate Publishing & Enterprises, LLC
127 E. Trade Center Terrace | Mustang, Oklahoma 73064 USA
1.888.361.9473 | www.tatepublishing.com

Tate Publishing is committed to excellence in the publishing industry. The company reflects the philosophy established by the founders, based on Psalm 68:11,
"The Lord gave the word and great was the company of those who published it."

Book design copyright © 2011 by Tate Publishing, LLC. All rights reserved.
Cover design by Amber Gulilat
Interior design by Christina Hicks

Published in the United States of America

ISBN: 978-1-61777-223-8
1. Biography & Autobiography / Law Enforcement
2. Biography & Autobiography / Women
11.07.12

Acknowledgments

First, I want to thank my heavenly Father for adopting me and showing me his amazing love. I want to thank Jesus for rescuing me from the darkness and calling me friend and many thanks to Holy Spirit for being an amazing teacher and guide. I would not be here without him.

Second, I would like to thank my good friend Debbie Sherman, who walked with me through some difficult times. I will be forever grateful for her prayers, words of encouragement, and help in getting the book started. She was my Jonathan when Saul was chasing me. I also would like to thank my friend Janet Schwind for her talents and support as she took my manuscript and laboriously worked to prepare it for submission. And to all my brothers and sisters in Christ who loved me right where I was while you shared God's love. I could not begin to list all of your names, but you know who you are and I just want to say, "Thank you!"

Last and most important, to all the men and women I served with on the police department protecting our community. Thank you for the honor of serving with you.

Table of Contents

When Desperation Meets Divinity, a Miracle Happens

> I gave up all that inferior stuff so I could know
> Christ personally, experience his resurrection
> power, be a partner in his suffering, and go all the
> way with him to death itself.
>
> Philippians 3:10–11

The rain beat down on my face as I looked up toward the dark storm clouds overhead. I cried out, "God, if you are real, I need you...I can't do this anymore." The rain mingled with my tears as I sat in the grass of my backyard holding a gun in my lap. Then I heard the familiar, ugly voice saying, "Go ahead. It's over. It's hopeless. Just do it." My trembling hand gripped the gun that was meant to protect in my role as a police officer and now was about to be leveled at my head.

My mind raced, my emotions raging with excruciating pain that was so deep it numbed me. I had finally come to that place in life called desperation. Maybe you have been there...that place of utter aloneness, a place where hope seems so distant and darkness threatens to overtake you, consume you. So there I was, in the world without God—hopeless and in need of a miracle. In a rush of memories, I realized I had spent all those years building my career on a foundation of sand. When the storm hit, of a magnitude that I was unprepared for, I watched as my career was torn apart by the onslaught of harsh elements raging against it.

How did I get here? What had gone wrong? Only a few months prior, which now seemed so long ago, I had been celebrating the news with my staff that I had come out number one on the Captain's Assessment Center. Balloons and cards adorned the office, and the sound of laughter filled the place. After the celebration died down and everyone had gone home that day, I remember sitting alone in my office amid the deadening silence, wondering why I felt so empty. After enduring seventeen grueling years of proving myself as a woman in this career field, I was finally about to accomplish my goal to become a captain on the police department. Through the years I had fought hard to earn all the degrees and the credentials to go with the title. So why was I unsatisfied? There had to be more than this. That hollow realization would eventually lead me to my knees in the rain and a divine encounter that would result in a miracle.

My career had become an idol in my life, and climbing the ladder of success was my singular motivation. On my way to the captain's position, I was presented with an opportunity that I thought would get me closer to my goal; instead, it would be used against me and result in my downfall. I remember the day I met with Paul, a deputy chief and the only one I trusted in this sheriff's administration. He informed me that he needed a replacement commander for the Community Relations Bureau, which was in his division. "Lieutenant," he said, "there are many morale and other problems in this bureau, so I am not promising it will be an easy transition." As we sat across from each other in the restaurant, I considered his offer and remembered that I had never shied away from any challenge before. Fighting back the fear rising inside of me, I accepted his offer.

The first day of my new assignment, I walked off the elevator and was immediately bombarded by the secretarial staff. "Lieutenant," they said, "we have been borrowing office supplies from another bureau in order to do our work. May we purchase supplies?"

I took a deep breath and replied, "Let me take a look at the budget, and I will let you know." My secretary, Judy, quickly retrieved the budget, which reflected a thirteen thousand dollar balance. I told the staff to order what they needed, and they were ecstatic. Even though the deputy chief had warned me about the condition of the bureau, I had no idea just how bad it was. The offices were overcrowded and disorganized, the carpet was filthy, and the walls needed a fresh coat of paint. The office equipment, an old green military color, looked like it came from the 1960s.

My first week I held a staff meeting to introduce myself, and as I sat down, one of the officers yelled out, "Lieutenant, don't sit on that chair!" I stopped just in time to look down and see the broken leg that was propped underneath the chair. I was so glad the officer had warned me so that I did not have to look up at them from the floor. I met all the employees that day and informed them that I was there to help get the bureau running effectively again and would need their help. I got a commitment from everyone, and they looked forward to having the Community Relations Bureau back on the chart.

There was no transition process with the previous commander, who was interested only in himself and his position as captain. My staff informed me that he'd spent his time in his office playing on the computer and running his personal business on the side. I saw evidence of his neglect everywhere I turned. Grant monies went untracked, and employees went unsupervised. In-fighting between sections and a backlog of paperwork hampered the daily work flow.

There were three sections in our bureau: Crime Prevention, DARE, and Youth Diversion. It shocked me to find out that the employees who worked in Youth Diversion were working without a contract. A grant had initially funded the program, and the previous commander had failed to complete the necessary paperwork to make them permanent employees. I had no sooner completed that arduous task when I was faced with another challenge. The task of turning the bureau around was monumental, but I rolled up my sleeves. And with the help of my hard-working staff, we jumped in. I took the money allotted in the new budget to purchase much-needed office equipment and prepared work orders to have the walls repainted and the carpet replaced. We selected modular furniture for each of the sections, which organized the space and provided private workspaces for employees. I called the two janitors assigned to our bureau and told them to bring a roll of large trash bags. I instructed every employee to throw away anything that was not being used. They found documents dating back to the 1960s. The janitors hauled off over a dozen trash bags stuffed with junk.

As the bureau began to take shape, the employees saw the effort that was being made on their behalf. As a result, arguing and in-fighting sharply declined. The office was now professional in appearance and much more conducive to a high level of productivity. The morale problem had been resolved, with the exception of two senior sergeants who had been in the bureau for years. They had run the show for a long time, so you can imagine the resistance when I began to hold them accountable and lay down the rules.

Chuck, the crime prevention sergeant, was especially problematic. He regularly flooded my inbox with memorandums for frivolous items and failed to meet deadlines in important areas. He scheduled his people for overtime when we did not have the funds in the budget, and then he would make it look like I was the bad guy. He was always testing me. One day he told me he found two of his employees locked together in a storage closet after hours and wanted to know what he should do about it. I asked him what department policy was and told him to follow it. I would soon find out how manipulative Chuck was.

Chuck constantly came into my office asking questions about my personal life. When I told him my personal life was none of his business, his attitude quickly changed from curiosity to hatred. I also discovered Chuck was good friends with the undersheriff and had influence with other high-ranking officers of the department.

When Chuck's animosity and dissension began to affect his performance, I placed him on written notice and gave him ninety days to improve. He promptly went over my head to my deputy chief and demanded my transfer. When the chief refused to transfer me, Chuck filed a gender discrimination complaint with the department's Diversity Office, of which he was a member and then spent his work time compiling a notebook of documentation to support his claim.

Karen, the police officer who held an offense against me, was now the head of the Diversity Office, and I knew she would not be objective. I discovered that Karen and Chuck conspired to stage a claim of retaliation, unbeknownst to me. I thought it was strangely coincidental when Deputy Chief Paul was suddenly transferred and replaced by another chief who despised me. Mike, the new deputy chief, was a good friend of the captain I had filed a discrimination complaint against. I found myself surrounded by my enemies. I worked under a tremendous amount of pressure, as I was continually challenged by Chuck's undermining tactics and intimidation as he continued to put together a case against me.

Chuck knew I was preparing to take the captain's promotional exam, so he took advantage of this opportunity to make his run at me. He continually came into my office unannounced at the end the day, attempting to engage me in casual conversations so he could covertly record them. He spoke misleadingly about not wanting to be transferred from the bureau. This went on for months with Chuck baiting me on transfer issues. He would later produce only the tapes that supported his discrimination claim and withhold all the other tapes—an illegal tactic known as entrapment. The tape he used to support his claim of retaliation featured me saying to Chuck that it was time for him to go because he had caused enough problems in the bureau. That statement taken out of context was the evidence the department used to support his claim of retaliation. Chuck continued to provoke me; the day we had a bureau photo shoot he showed up wearing a bright orange shirt with a gaudy necktie. Some of the officers laughed, even though they knew Chuck was pushing it. I was prevented from disciplining Chuck for his misconduct by the new deputy chief, who, unbeknownst to me, was setting me up for a fall.

Prior to the captain's exam, I was approached by two homosexual lieutenants, Terrie and Mark, who wanted me to join them in promoting their agenda on the police department. They too were members of the Diversity Board and had been instrumental in getting sexual orientation added to the discrimination policy. They assured me that being associated with them would be my ticket to command staff. I declined their offer, saying, "I fly solo, and the only way I want to be promoted is based on my merit, not someone's agenda." That comment did not go over well with them, and they would have an opportunity to get back at me when they voted on the retaliation case.

I took the captain's promotional exam in January 1997, and, to everyone's surprise, I came out number one. My deputy chief had brought in an outside consulting agency to run the assessment center, so there was no way the department could manipulate the scores. The sheriff was livid when he found out where I was ranked, and the pressure intensified when Chuck and my deputy chief filed another complaint against me with Internal Affairs. I endured a grueling month-long investigation that involved all of my employees and brought the bureau's operations to a standstill.

During this time I was stopped by two deputy chiefs who asked if I had heard the sheriff was freezing the captain's promotional list. I immediately got a sick feeling in my stomach when I realized the sheriff would stop at nothing to prevent my promotion, even if it meant demoting me. My chief, who oversaw the Diversity Office, allowed Chuck to remain in the bureau from January through June while he compiled evidence from his covert tape recordings.

I found out about the recordings when my secretary Judy came into my office one afternoon, sobbing and obviously upset. She tearfully shared what had been going on. Chuck had called her into his office when I was on vacation, revealing to Judy his lower leg and the minicassette recorder discreetly taped to it. He boasted that he had been taping me and was going to wait and see what his evaluation looked like before he turned the tapes over. He arrogantly pointed to a duffle back sitting next to his desk that contained numerous cassette tapes.

I immediately contacted the district attorney's office, Civil Division, to get a legal opinion on covert tape recording. They informed me that it was legal to tape record in the state of Nevada, as long as it was face to face. The attorney said, "It's really a gray area of the law, and although it is not illegal, it is highly unethical." I got a written memorandum from the head of the division that recommended the tapes be turned over to Internal Affairs and the sergeant investigated. This memorandum I delivered to my deputy chief, who put it in his drawer and said, "That's all, Lieutenant. You're dismissed." Next I completed Chuck's evaluation after speaking with the chief about the low rating I planned to give Chuck.

"Do you want to be a captain?" the chief asked me. I nodded, and he said, "Then you will straight-line him and let it go!" He was ordering me to rate Chuck as meeting department standards and ignoring the disciplinary problems that occurred during that year; this completely went against my principles, and I was sickened by it. I knew I was in a no-win situation: if I complied with his orders it would at some time down the road be used against me, and if I did not, he would see to it that I was not promoted to captain. Against my conscience, I rated Chuck as meeting standards in all areas of performance and sent it to the chief's office for approval.

I have never worked around someone as evil as I felt this chief to be. I thought back to the time when he was my sergeant in patrol and having an affair. Now this same man sat in judgment of me. Within thirty days I was called into his office and placed on administrative leave, pending an investigation for retaliation. I stood there in unbelief and asked, "What do you mean retaliation?"

Karen and another lieutenant, Greg, said, "We will be investigating allegations that you retaliated against Chuck for filing a discrimination complaint against you."

"That is ridiculous!" I responded. The chief stepped in and relieved me of duty, ordering me off the property. I was told to remain at my residence between business hours, available for call, and I was admonished not to contact anyone in the department. I was in complete shock. I don't even remember the drive home that day.

My career had been my whole life. Being a police officer had become my identity—it was who I was and all I was. Now I was lost without it. I had never been under investigation for any violation before and had an impeccable performance as an officer. The reason I was in this situation was clear—I had stood up against the good old boy network, and I would pay dearly. I was confined to my home in isolation as I waited for the department to notify me of my interview. An overwhelming fear overtook me—mentally, physically, emotionally—as I faced the possibility of losing my career. Finally, after I was at home for two months, not allowed to work, they called me in to report for an interview. At the department I entered a cold, sterile room where Greg and Karen, the two Diversity Board investigators, sat silently behind the table in the center of the room. I took my seat facing them, and the interrogation began. Over the next four hours they badgered me with questions about specific conversations that I did not remember and then accused me of lying because I did not recall details. Their evidence was the tape recordings that I was never given access to, which put me at a tremendous disadvantage. I was not allowed to take a break. Finally, when I was unable to talk any longer, they shut off the recorder. My head was swirling, and my body trembled from the stress I was under. I tried not to show it to my interrogators.

Karen and Greg were merciless as they accused me of retaliating against Chuck, and they refused to accept the fact that I was following an order from my chief. The evaluation I had been coerced into completing was used against me as evidence, just as I had feared. If this had been an actual criminal case, the evidence used against me and the method of interrogation would have qualified as entrapment, and the case would have been thrown out of court. That, however, would not be the case in my situation. After I had endured the four-hour interrogation, they sarcastically asked, "Do you have any questions, Lieutenant?"

I looked into their cold, dark eyes and replied, "Why are you doing this?"

"You're dismissed, Lieutenant," they said with no emotion, and turned away. I drove away, beating my steering wheel angrily and choking back uncontrollable sobs. When I got home, emotionally exhausted, I fell into my bed and woke up the next morning still wearing the clothes I had worn to the interview. I looked in the mirror and did not recognize the disheveled, battered person looking back at me. My appearance reflected the hopeless condition of my heart, and I knew this was it.

I went outside and sat down in my backyard as the rain pelted me. Trembling, I lifted the gun to my head. I just wanted it to be over. As the gun touched my temple and I poised to carry out an irreversible act, my pug, Cagney, ran to me, startling me out of my stupor and interrupting the very moment I was about to pull the trigger. The next few moments are a blur. It is still a mystery how my dog got out of the house, and I have trouble recalling how I got back into my house. I just remember falling into bed, exhausted by the traumatic ordeal.

When I awoke, it was pitch black in my room, and I had no idea how long I had slept. Suddenly—before I had time to realize what had just happened to me—an amazing golden light filled my room, and I began to sense powerful waves of peace and love washing over me. I got down on my knees and began to weep. The Bible says that it is God's kindness that leads to repentance, and one moment in his presence would change my life. I had never felt such an overwhelming sense of love and peace. I instinctively reached over and picked up the Bible my brother had given me and read what he had written on the inside cover. It said, "Deb, I hope this opportunity to read this helps confirm that we have a loving Father and friend that loves us so much that He died rather than face eternity without us." He wrote John 3:16, which says, "This is how much God loved the world: He gave his Son, his one and only Son. And this is why: so that no one need be destroyed; by believing in him, anyone can have a whole and lasting life."

At that moment I was confronted with truth and captivated by love as tears of repentance streamed down my face. It was in that desperate place that the cry of my heart was heard by my Creator, and I was instantly translated from the kingdom of darkness into his glorious light. Jesus explained what I had just experienced to Nicodemus, a prominent religious leader in his time, when he said in John 3:3, "Unless a person is born from above, it's not possible to see what I'm pointing to—to God's kingdom." In a moment, the miracle of salvation had occurred. I suddenly realized that this divine encounter with our loving Creator had occurred on August 5, 1997.

In God's numbering system, eight represents new beginnings, and the number five symbolizes grace. This marked forty years that I had been living in the kingdom of darkness, and by God's grace I became a new creation with a brand new beginning. It is by grace that we are saved through something called faith; it is nothing that we can do for ourselves. It is a gift of God. Even though it looked like my life was hopelessly out of control, God was in complete control and had allowed these circumstances to bring me into my destiny.

So what happened that day in the rain? How did my dog get out, and how did I get into my house? The answer came a few weeks later when I was informed that I had been demoted to sergeant. I also was suffering from Post Traumatic Stress Syndrome and put on medical leave by my doctor. He prescribed rest and relaxation, so I headed to Chicago to visit my sister and her family. It was then that I got my answer.

As I walked up the aisle to get off the plane, someone called out, "Debra!" I looked over to see a man with a warm glowing countenance sitting in the window seat. "God bless you," he said simply.

I smiled and responded, "Thank you." Then it hit me. How did that man know my name? It wasn't written anywhere, and I had not talked to anyone. I heard a small voice inside me say, "My angels helped you that day; you're not alone." I almost fell to my knees when I realized that God was talking to me; the hair stood up on my neck as I felt his presence. I was not familiar with his voice as it was much different than the ugly voice

"What Have I Gotten Myself Into?"

God met me more than halfway, he freed me from
my anxious fears.

Psalm 34:4

It all started my senior year of college when I came across a
recruiting ad for the Las Vegas Metropolitan Police Department.
I remember staring at the ad, wondering if this was what I was
meant to do. I was intrigued with the idea of being a police officer and putting my life on the line to protect others. It seemed
like an honorable profession, and it appealed to my sense of
adventure and desire to make a difference in my community. So
I answered the ad, not fully knowing what I was getting myself
into. But do we ever really know?

I reported to the Police Academy on a Saturday morning
and lined up with hundreds of male applicants who were competing for the fifty academy positions. The first round of testing
consisted of a written examination requiring a score of seventy
or higher. I took the test, and a few weeks later I received a letter
informing me I had successfully completed the first portion of
the test, with a written score in the high nineties. I grabbed the
letter and showed my mother, who shared in my excitement.

My next hurdle was the physical fitness test, which was held
at the firearms range. At the time, I was competing in long-
distance running, so I decided—perhaps naively—to run the five

miles to the course as my warm-up training run. When I jogged up to the parking lot, I saw a large group of men and a couple of women lined up awaiting their turn to run the obstacle course. I also noticed an ambulance team standing by. I took my place in line to await my turn.

The drill sergeant called my name when I was next to go, and I found myself standing behind a man twice my size. For this portion of the test we were required to run a four hundred-yard obstacle course in under one hundred seconds. When the starter's gun went off, the man in front of me took off sprinting to the first obstacle—a drainage pipe about three feet high and fifteen feet long. I watched as he crawled through the pipe successfully. But then as he began to run again, he failed to lift his head and struck the next obstacle a few feet away headfirst. He was knocked out cold. I watched as the ambulance crew loaded him on a gurney and took him away.

"Gauthier, you're up!" the drill sergeant yelled. I jogged up to the line and squatted down in a sprinter's stance. When the gun went off, I raced to the drainage pipe. Because of my small stature I was able to bend over and run right through it without any problems. When I came out of the pipe, I sprinted to the next obstacle, a six-foot block wall, and blithely ran up and over. On the other side was a rope that I had to quickly climb and use to swing over a trench. Then I ran to the next obstacle, a small retainer wall, which I easily leapt over in full stride. And finally, the last obstacle…another six-foot block wall. Pumped on adrenaline, I climbed it and then onto the roof of a building, as just then the sergeant hit the stopwatch and called time.

The leading time was seventy-six seconds, run by a university football player. The sergeant shook his head in disbelief as he looked at his stopwatch and then at me; my time was eighty-three seconds, he said. That caught the attention of the other candidates, and they watched in amazement as I jogged home.

Looking back, running home after that arduous test of endurance was not the wisest thing to do, but I was young and did not care what they thought. As I ran, a car pulled up beside me driven by a heavyset man wearing a light blue polyester suit that was stretched tautly over his big belly. As he chomped on his cigar, he asked in a southern drawl, "Are you one of them there marathon runners?" I laughed and thought to myself, *Who is this guy?* I later found out he was the commander of personnel, who took it upon himself to inform the academy staff that a female marathon runner was entering the academy and would run their socks off.

The next stage of testing was the oral boards, where we would appear before a panel of officers and answer practical questions. The day of the test, an officer led me into a lobby, where I sat with several men dressed in business suits. I fit right in with my navy blue suit and crisp white blouse, minus the heels. While awaiting our turns, we heard a commotion inside the interview room. Next thing you know, two officers emerged, holding up the recruit by his arms. Evidently he had fainted under the pressure; he was still disoriented and sweating. At this point, again, I wondered what I had gotten myself into.

When my turn came, a six-foot-five motorcycle sergeant wearing big black boots opened the door for me to enter. Once inside the room, I saw two mean-looking officers sitting behind a table with a single chair in the center of the room facing them. The officer who invited me in directed the first question at me, followed by the others, who challenged every answer I gave. I firmly stood my ground, even when asked about the outcome of a hypothetical robbery in progress. When I told the panel that I had chased the armed suspect and apprehended him, they quickly challenged me, insisting I was not able to catch him and that now he was barricaded in a grocery store and had taken hostages. I respectfully replied that I had captured him before he made it into the store and told the panel to look at my running time. The sergeant looked at my file and laughed, saying, "Okay, we'll give you that one." I guess they liked my boldness and tenacity, because I passed the orals with a score in the nineties.

Several months later I received a letter from the police department informing me I had successfully completed all the testing and had come out at the top of the list. I was scheduled to attend the next academy that would start on November 28, 1980, with an all-day orientation, followed by four months of intense training. I was excited and scared at the same time, as my dream of being a police officer began to unfold; I knew there was no turning back now.

The week leading up to the academy orientation was extremely busy. First stop, county hospital for my physical exam. I remember standing in the cold, sterile hallway waiting to have my blood drawn and then reporting to the cardiologist to undergo a treadmill test. I also completed a pulmonary test to reveal lung capacity, a hearing test, X-rays, and finally, a complete physical done by an old medical doctor who asked me if I was sure I knew what I was getting into. I told him of course I was sure, and he smiled, signing me off on the last portion of the testing.

The next stop was the uniform shop, where I was measured for my uniforms by a seamstress named Alice. She was the first person to actually encourage me. We both laughed as she told me jokes about men. As I stood in front of the mirror wearing the smallest men's uniform she could find, we both laughed because I looked like a little kid, with sleeves past my fingertips, pants dragging on the ground, and the necktie hanging between my legs. My five-foot-three, 108-pound frame was going to be a challenge in the uniform department, but Alice went the extra mile to custom fit my uniforms. I later picked up four dress uniforms, two khaki utility uniforms, sweats, running gear, and a dress hat and baseball cap. While she was tailoring my uniform, I completed it by purchasing a pair of black boots and cleaning supplies.

My final stop that week was to the Clark County Courthouse, where I would be sworn in as a police officer. I will never forget that day as I proudly stood in my police uniform for photos and the official swearing-in. That was the day I dedicated my life to a career as a police officer. I raised my right hand and repeated after the clerk the Law Enforcement Code of Ethics:

> As a Law Enforcement Officer, my fundamental duty is to serve mankind; to safeguard lives and property; to protect the innocent against deception, the weak against oppression or intimidation, and the peaceful against violence or disorder; and to respect the Constitutional rights of all men to liberty, equality, and justice. I will keep my private life unsullied as an example to all; maintain courageously calm in the face of danger, scorn or ridicule; develop self-restraint; and be constantly mindful of the welfare of others. Honest in thought and deed in both my personal and official life, I will be exemplary to obeying the laws of the land and regulations of my department. Whatever I see or hear of a confidential nature or that is confided to me in my official capacity will be kept ever secret unless revelation is necessary in the performance of my duty. I will never act officiously or permit my personal feelings, prejudices, animosities, or friendships to influence my decision. With no compromise for crime and with relentless prosecution of criminals, I will enforce the law courteously and appropriately without fear, or favor, malice or ill will, never employing unnecessary force or violence and never accepting gratuities. I recognize

the badge of my office as a symbol of public faith, and will accept it as a public trust to be held so long as I am true to the ethics of the police service. I will constantly strive to achieve these objectives and ideals, dedicating myself before God to my chosen profession—law enforcement.

I don't know if I really understood the tremendous responsibility that went along with the badge and what I would have to endure to earn the right to wear it.

The day I had eagerly waited for finally arrived as I joined forty-nine other recruits for a day of orientation to prepare us for the start of the academy. I stood in the brisk November morning air, holding my uniforms and box of supplies as I visibly shook from a combination of fear and cold.

All of a sudden, one of the academy officers came out of the building yelling commands and calling us all manner of demeaning names. They rushed us into a classroom where three other crew-cut military-looking men barked orders at us. As I entered the classroom, I saw my nameplate next to a row of other names, my books neatly stacked behind it. I quickly sat down and kept my eyes fixed on the front of the room, not wanting to draw attention to myself.

When the academy sergeant entered the room, we immediately jumped to attention. He told us to look to our left and then said, "That person will not be here at the end of this training!" I don't know if the sergeant had a crystal ball, but we lost fifty percent of our class before it was over.

My attempt to go unnoticed was futile as the sergeant walked over to me, grabbing my waist-long hair, and yelled, "What is this, Gauthier?"

I was going to say, "Hair, sir!" but decided to remain quiet.

The sergeant growled and said, "Gauthier, you will have that hair cut off by Monday morning. Do you understand?"

"Yes, sir!" I yelled out. He then leaned over and whispered in my ear, "You better be #@%* good because I don't believe girls belong here!" A chill went down my spine, and I kept my eyes straight ahead, not daring to respond.

On a stress meter from one to ten, this day was a fifteen as the academy officers bombarded us with information in between the yelling and screaming. We were responsible for everything we were being told in preparation for Monday morning. It was now time to open the box that contained my duty weapon, holster, belt, handcuffs, baton, mace, and cleaning supplies. We carefully removed each item, and, following the instructions of the officer, we put together our utility belt. When I got all the items on my belt, they filled every inch of it because my waist was so small.

Another academy officer instructed us in breaking down and reassembling the duty weapon. I listened carefully and followed each step as I took apart the Smith and Wesson 9mm pistol. We then had two minutes to reassemble the gun at his command. When he whistled, I frantically began to reassemble the gun and forgot which parts went together and in what order. The whistle blew again, and we were instructed to place the weapon on the table in front of us as the academy officers inspected them. When they got to me and saw my weapon unassembled, they ordered me to do push-ups as the academy officers laughed and told the others what a disappointment I was going to be at the range.

After lunch, we assembled in the parking lot where we were taught military formations and marching orders. We spent the afternoon practicing these drills in order to be prepared for inspection Monday morning. Several of my classmates were selected for class sergeant and platoon officers. These were the lead positions for the inspection, and each of us would follow their commands so that we moved as a unit in complete precision and timing. After several hours of practice, we were ordered back into the classroom and finally dismissed. My day would not end for many hours as I doggedly ensured that every part of my uniform met the highest standards—uniform meticulously pressed, boots and leather gear spit-shined so thoroughly that I could see my reflection in them. I had watched my father do this when he was in the military, so I was familiar with the process.

My first stop on Saturday morning was the hair salon to have my hair cut in a military style: above the ears and not touching the collar. As I watched my hair fall to the ground, the tears welled up in my eyes because I had always worn my hair long. Now I looked in shock at my reflection and did not recognize myself. It felt strange to run my fingers through just a few inches of hair. I felt naked. The rest of the weekend was spent memorizing police codes and law enforcement definitions that had to be recited from memory during inspection. I jumped into the reading assignments, though as an art major in college they were all very foreign to me. If there was ever going to be a makeover, this would qualify, as I went from the free-spirit artist to Robo Cop!

For the next four months I attended the academy from six a.m. to five p.m., Monday through Friday. Each morning we stood inspection for approximately forty-five minutes. I found that being short was an advantage—the academy officers looked right over my head so I did not have to stare at them, which made it easier to recite my definitions as I focused on their tie tacks. The rest of the day was spent taking classes on criminal law, police procedures, and a host of other topics. In addition to academics, we had practical problems that included instruction on making vehicle and people stops, handling crimes in progress, and solving problems related to high-risk situations. At the end of the day we endured physical training, which included a three- to five-mile run with wind sprints and calisthenics at intervals in between.

On Monday morning the alarm went off at 4:30 a.m. I jumped out of bed and into the shower as I prepared for the first day of the police academy. I arrived with my classmates at six a.m. to prepare for inspection. After changing into my uniform in the locker room, I joined the men outside as we inspected one another, cutting stray strings from our uniforms and pulling off any lint. We wore our dress uniforms with hat and gloves and I sported my gleaming new boots and leather gear on which I had spent so many hours.

After many practice runs through the inspection drills, we all stood at attention as we waited for the academy staff. The sun was just coming up as I stood in the brisk morning air, trying not to tremble from the cold and fear. At eight a.m. sharp, the doors of the academy building swung open, and the staff marched out. When the sergeant reached us, the class sergeant did a crisp about-face and yelled, "Class, prepare for inspection!" We grabbed our firearms from the holster in unison and stood at attention with weapons in front of our chest. As the academy sergeant began to inspect the class sergeant, the officers marched toward the platoon leaders to begin their inspections.

There was much yelling, with recruits dropping to do push-ups or run laps around the parking lot, referred to as the "grinder." The officer assigned to my platoon finally approached me, and I stood firmly as he asked me the definition of a crime. As I recited the definition, he violently yanked the pistol out of my hand and began to inspect it with his white glove. He interrupted me, yelling, "Gauthier, drop and give me twenty-five pushups for having a hairball in your weapon!"

At the end of the twenty-five pushups, I yelled, "Sir, Recruit Gauthier requests permission to recover!" He left me there for a while as my arms trembled under my body weight.

Finally, when I could no longer hold myself up, he yelled, "Recover!" He continued with the inspection, and I received demerits or "gigs" as they were called, for my weapon and a string that he called a "rope" hanging from my uniform. We were allowed only a certain number of gigs during the course of training, and if we exceeded that number, we would be dismissed (or as they called it "washed out").

The first couple of weeks, each inspection lasted more than an hour. Every day we became more and more proficient at the drills, and our preparation time was reduced. I was forced to cut my hair several times during that first week because it was not to the satisfaction of the academy sergeant. I was horrified when I had to keep returning to my hair stylist to tell him my hair was not short enough. From that point on I hid my hair under my ball cap when I wasn't in class. After inspection we entered the classroom and began the academic portion of the academy. Officers ordered us to take meticulous hand-printed notes on each class; these notes would be inspected for accuracy and neatness. At the beginning of each week we were given an exam covering all the material we had received the preceding week and were required to maintain a 70 percent average.

After classes were complete the class sergeant ordered us to dress out for physical training. We had approximately five minutes to fall out in the parking lot in inspection formation. The academy was located across the street from a park where we did all of our physical training drills. We began the session with calisthenics and stretching, and then ran in formation around the park while we chanted, "We are Metro, the mighty, mighty Metro...everywhere we go people want to know, who we are, what we stand for." We would repeat this many times while doing our three- to five-mile run.

The first week, the officers ordered us to sit in a large circle while the sergeant called out the names of two recruits who were told to sit back to back in the center of the circle. When the whistle blew, the recruits would wrestle for two minutes and try to pin the other before time was called. After several men had gone through the drill, the sergeant yelled, "Gauthier and

Gillespie, you're up!" I pressed my back against the recruit, who was much larger than I was.

When the whistle blew, I immediately rolled over and grabbed him between the legs, hard. He let out a blood-curdling scream as I held on and squeezed until time was called. The sergeant smiled and said, "Good job, Gauthier," as the male recruit complained that I had cheated. The sergeant said to the class, "There's no fair fight on the streets; you fight to win!"

I excelled in the academy and was at the top of my class academically as well as physically. This did not sit well with many of the male recruits, who began to harass me. One morning before inspection, a male recruit named Dillon whistled at me while I walked down the hallway. He would often tell filthy sexual jokes in front of me while we were waiting for inspection. The sergeant heard Dillon whistle at me and jumped all over him, which only added to the resentment and anger that these men had toward me.

During one inspection a male recruit forgot his weapon on the locker room bench. It was picked up by one of the academy officers, who replaced it with a dildo. The recruit was humiliated during inspection when he was handed this object and ordered to carry it in his holster throughout the week. When we stood at inspection, this poor guy had to hold the dildo like he was holding his gun. I found it extremely offensive and was embarrassed for him and me, but I dared not say anything. Dillon and his buddies thought it was cute to grab the dildo from the recruit's holster and rub it against my leg while making groaning noises and vulgar sexual comments. I called him a pig and told him to leave me alone, but he would just laugh and continue his vulgar behavior.

As the weeks became months, I watched as many of my classmates washed out of the academy for various reasons. On a day that someone was going to be kicked out, academy officers would place a cutout of a black hand in the one-way mirrored window that separated their office from our classroom; that day would be become known as "Black Monday" for instance, and we sweated, not knowing who would be washing out.

The academy officers would march into the classroom carrying a glass aquarium and a cage full of mice that represented us in number. The aquarium housed Doctor Doom, a large boa constrictor that sat coiled in the tank. We watched as the officer would calmly grab one of the mice from the cage and drop it into the glass tank. It would leap to the top of the tank and shake frantically from fear as Doctor Doom began to slowly move in on its prey. The staff would then leave us to watch the demise of the little mouse, which represented one of us who was about to "meet our doom." I recall sitting there with sweat beaded on my forehead as we waited for the staff to return. After several minutes they would march in, approach the unsuspecting recruit, and snatch his books from the desk, ordering him to follow them to his office. I would later see the "wash out" walking down the hallway with gear in hand and teary eyed. It was an insensitive and demeaning way of dismissing someone, and recruits who could not take the pressure would voluntarily resign.

Midpoint in the academy we participated in a two-week ride-along with a field training officer. I was grateful to ride with an officer named Ron, who was very sympathetic to women working in patrol. After briefing, I followed Ron out to the patrol car, and he went through the checkout procedure with me. I was so excited about the ride-along that I had not slept the night before, and I arrived at the station several hours early to get ready for my first night on patrol. I worked the swing shift from three p.m. to one a.m.

While on patrol I was all eyes, and my heart jumped when I spotted some suspicious activity. "Sir, stop!" I yelled to Ron, "I just saw a guy back there lifting a television out of a side window." Ron spun the police car around, turning off our lights, and we quickly exited the car and snuck up on two men who were burglarizing a house. Ron pulled his gun on the burglars and yelled at them to get down on the ground. When they complied, Ron gave me the privilege of using my felony handcuffing technique to immobilize them as he covered me with his gun.

The people who lived at the house were out for the evening, so when they returned we took a police report. Meanwhile the burglars were arrested and transported to jail; I had made my first felony arrest! Ron and I were the talk of the station when we got in that night, and he was really proud of me. I was so high from adrenalin that I didn't sleep that night either. I knew then that all the challenges and pain I had endured were worth it, and this was what I was designed to do.

When we returned to the academy the following week, officers instructed us to write a thirty-page term paper summarizing our patrol experience. I had many exciting things to write about, and my effort paid off when my paper received the top score. As a result, I was made class sergeant for the twelfth week of the academy and earned extra leadership points toward my final score. My excitement was short lived when one of the recruits who had not completed the assignment decided to cheat by putting blank paper in-between several typed pages. He assumed the staff would not read all the papers, but he was wrong. When the officers came out to inspection in their physical training uniform, I knew we were in trouble! They commanded us to fall out for a five-mile run in full dress uniform through the neighboring streets. We ran with our batons at port arms, and it wasn't long before my arms were burning from the weight and position. My boots were still very new and had not been broken in completely, so naturally I began to develop blisters on both my feet. When we made it back to the academy we were ordered into the park, where we ran wind sprints until we could not run anymore.

When it was finally over, I limped into the locker room and pulled off my boots, only to find my socks stuck to bloody blisters on my feet. As I washed the blood off my feet, the sergeant yelled, "Recruits, front and center!" We were ushered into the classroom, where we stood at attention for several hours as sweat ran down my face and my feet swelled in my boots.

This became a "Black Hand Day" and we were required to do more physical training at day's end to break us further. With swollen bloody feet, I wobbled around the park in a "duck walk," which caused my thighs and calves to cramp. At the end we did wind sprints again until many of the recruits were throwing up. I don't know how I was able to make it to the locker room, but when I did, I broke down in tears.

By then we had lost almost half of the class, and only one other woman of the five who'd started remained. Her name was Lois, and she was very masculine and vocal with the men. Three weeks before graduation, Lois, the class sergeant, had a run-in with one of the male recruits who would not follow her commands. She was overheard by the academy staff telling this recruit that she would not back him if he were the last cop on the planet. They promptly fired her for that comment without explanation. She was devastated, and I thought, if they fired her they would probably fire me. So I continued to keep my mouth shut and do all that was required to make it through. Being the only woman left in the academy significantly increased my sense of isolation. The sergeant didn't help matters either when he entered the classroom to tell the male recruits that I was beating them academically and especially on the firearms range, where my average was 98 percent. Even though I had never fired a pistol and still had difficulty putting it back together, I discovered that size and strength were irrelevant when it came to accuracy. Firing was all about finesse and focus, and I carefully followed the instruction of the range master. This increased my level of

Debra Gauthier

confidence, because I knew that my firearm would be the equalizer on the street. The target shooting was dynamic in nature and simulated shooting situations that we would face on the streets. We would run through an obstacle course while engaging the targets and making split-second decisions whether to shoot or not. Accuracy, timing, and decision-making were tested during these drills.

Another aspect of training was called "practical problems," which simulated activities that tested our knowledge of patrol procedures and problem-solving abilities, as well as our reaction under pressure. For instance, the first problem involved stopping a suspicious person: the stop was comprised of safety tactics, interview skills, and problem-solving. We had to determine what the person was doing and establish their true identity using all the resources we had available to us. The practical problems increased in difficulty as we progressed in our training.

The last problem we faced was a felony situation involving a crime in progress. I sat in my patrol car with a training officer sitting in the back seat, who would grade me, as a car sped by shooting blanks in my direction! I took this as my cue and pressed down on the accelerator in pursuit of the vehicle down a dark, remote street. As I chased the car with my red lights flashing and siren blaring, the passenger continued to fire rounds at me. I grabbed the radio mike to give the dispatcher my direction of travel, location, and a description of the vehicle, when she responded that there was no backup available. I thought, *You have got to be kidding, lady!*

Before I could initiate a stop, the vehicle pulled to a stop alongside a dark road. I quickly exited the patrol car, pointing my shotgun at the passengers inside. I ordered the driver out at gunpoint and observed a huge male with his hands in the air get out of the driver's side. I yelled at him to get on the ground as I watched the passenger, and when he was stretched out on the pavement I ordered the passenger out. I had to rely on the spotlight from my vehicle, as it was pitch black outside. When I had both suspects lying on the ground, my backup arrived and covered me as I approached the driver and began a pat-down search. I thoroughly searched all areas of this man for possible weapons and found a string hanging from his crotch area. "What's this?" I asked him. He laughed as I proceeded to rip open his trousers and remove a derringer from between his legs. The string was attached to the gun so he could easily pull it out and shoot me. I was one of the few recruits who spotted the weapon because I was not shy about grabbing this guy's crotch.

During the last week of the academy I was injured during the defensive tactics test. The officer in charge of defensive tactics stood six feet two inches and weighed two hundred and twenty pounds of solid muscle. In order to pass the practical exam, we had to defend ourselves with our baton as this huge man attacked us with an axe handle. When it was my turn to go, the first strike against my baton sent a numbing, searing pain down my forearm. He swung the handle again, and this time my baton flew out of my hand as the ligaments tore in my arm. I yelled out in pain and cussed the guy out in front of my classmates. They were all a little surprised, and at that point I didn't care because this guy had hurt me. I escaped to the locker room and ran my arm under the cold water as I choked back the tears.

I was ordered to go to the emergency room, where my wrist and forearm were found to be badly bruised and the ligaments strained. I left in a splint, and the doctor told me not to participate in physical training. I explained that I would be washed out of the academy and begged him to allow me to finish the class requirements wearing the brace. He reluctantly agreed and put "limited restrictions" on the doctor's note.

The next day was the most important and demanding of our sixteen weeks of training. It was known only to us as "survival day" and would be led by the department's SWAT team. This was the time in our training when we would have to apply all our knowledge and skills to survive at any cost. We sat in the classroom that morning, not knowing what to expect. My arm was in the splint and throbbing with pain when a group of SWAT officers burst into the classroom and opened fire. I dove behind the desk and returned fire, emptying my pistol and grabbing another magazine before the siege ended. We then headed out to the firearms range for a day of survival training. I was surprised that I was able to do as well as I did with one arm. The SWAT guys were impressed too, and they actually helped me in a couple of tight situations. That day I learned how to do a "spider drop" from a roof top, hanging from the roof by fingertips and toes. It was the funniest-looking thing, but very effective.

When the day was finally over, the male recruits mooned the SWAT officers as they drove away and then decided to "pants" me as their reward. I figured that I had survived ten hours of testing from highly skilled SWAT officers, so I looked at these guys as amateurs. I decided right there that no one was going to touch me. When a few brave souls attempted to get close, I wielded my baton and struck them as they came near. The first recruit yelled, "She's really hitting me!" They reluctantly decided to back off and turned their attention on one of the other male recruits.

Our training was drawing to a close, and this portion of the training had separated the "men from the boys." Since I did not fit into either category, I was not permitted to share in their victory celebration as they got inebriated in the parking lot. I went home that night to tend to my aching arm and the pain that I felt in my heart from knowing I would never truly be accepted by these men, no matter what I did. I came to terms with the fact that I was resented whether I did well or did poorly; the underlying message was that I was not welcome on their turf.

On March 28, 1981, I graduated in seventh place in my class, alongside twenty-seven male recruits, with a final score of 88.66 (with the top score being 91.29). I became the first woman hired under the same standards as the men and would join the ranks of other women who had been pioneers in their police departments. I would learn of the price that is paid by those who go before us; it was at times a difficult and lonely road to travel.

The field portion of our training was now ahead of us. We would be assigned to a patrol station, working with four different training officers over a period of four months, and be rated on our performance in addition to weekly written tests. I was assigned to the Southeast Area Command working the swing shift from three p.m. to one a.m. On my first day I sat in a crowded briefing room full of male officers, waiting to be introduced to my training officer. The sergeant briefed us on recent crimes and outstanding suspect information as well as changes in procedures and other information pertinent to patrol. At the end of the briefing the officers cleared out, and I was left in the room alone. I went out to the parking lot and saw a stocky officer with a snarl on this face. I somehow knew this was my training officer, even though he had not bothered to introduce himself.

I did not let his demeanor shake me, and I approached him, standing by as he checked out the car. Ed, my training officer, was old enough to be my father. It reminded me of when I was a little girl and I asked my dad if I could help him fix the car. He would always say, "Sure, just don't touch anything." I felt the same way now with Ed. Unlike Ron, my first partner who wanted me to succeed, Ed was irritated that I had been assigned to him, and I knew I would have to prove myself. He finally threw the other set of car keys at me, and I got into the passenger side of the vehicle.

Ed did not speak to me for the entire first week. He just grumbled when he was hungry and we had not yet been cleared for dinner. I figured out that I was to get on the radio and ask the dispatcher to clear us for dinner. The first night I forgot to turn my portable radio off when I keyed the microphone, which caused a loud squeal on the car radio. Ed cringed and punched me squarely in the arm. Every time I made this mistake, Ed would repeat this punishment until my arm was so sore I told him I couldn't take it anymore. The next time it happened, Ed hit me in my thigh, causing my muscle to spasm; I just could not win with this guy.

Ed was a fifteen-year veteran officer, and, quirks aside, I was fortunate to have him as my training officer, because he was a master at conducting narcotics investigations. He made a project of closing down the drug paraphernalia shops in our area, so I learned advanced police skills, like how to conduct surveillances and put together search warrants. One night we were extremely busy running from call to call; it was after ten p.m., and we still had not been cleared for dinner when we got a call of a suspicious circumstance. Ed grunted, knowing it was going to be a while before we could eat, as I reached for the mike and told the dispatcher we were enroute. She informed us that two truck drivers were overheard talking over their CB radios about a dead body in the swamp area. We had no other information, so Ed assumed it was bogus, and he was not happy that dinner was again delayed.

Upon arriving at a dark swamp area on the city's outskirts, Ed shocked me when he parked the car, reclined in his seat, and said, "Go check it out, rookie!" I began my investigation walking up the road, flashlight in hand, as the frogs croaked loudly in the black night. It was eerie, and I was reminded of those horror movies I had seen where the creature comes out of the lagoon and grabs the unsuspecting victim. I shook off my thoughts and continued up the road, briefly looking back at the police car with its "redheads" flashing in the distance when I spotted an odd-looking round object in a shallow stream running adjacent to the road. I carefully walked down the slope from the road to investigate. I picked up a stick and used it to roll the rock over; I was horrified when a patch of hair fell over the face of a man contorted with fear. He had been decapitated by some jagged tool, and the water in the stream had preserved his face. I stifled the scream that wanted to come out of me and grabbed my gun, pointing it at the dark shadows in the bushes behind me.

I quickly calmed myself and regained my composure as I backed out of the area, stepping in my original footprints, careful not to destroy any evidence and preserve the crime scene. I ran back to the police car and swung open the passenger door as I tried to catch my breath, shouting, "Sir, there is a man's head over there!"

My mouth dropped open when Ed, not moving from his reclined position, replied, "Well, go get the @#%* thing and bring it back here so we can go to lunch!" I just sat there with my mouth hanging open when Ed finally sat up and smiled, saying, "Let's see what you've got." I showed him the crime scene, and he roped off the area with yellow tape. We began a grid search, looking for the body as we waited for the arrival of homicide detectives and crime scene analysts. After several hours at the crime scene, we never did get a chance to eat dinner. We later learned that the victim had been reported missing by his wife, and his truck was found a few days earlier abandoned and set on fire. Three weeks later his headless body was found in the foothills of the mountains. He had been the victim of a violent murder scheme orchestrated by his wife and her boyfriend.

At the end of the shift I walked into the briefing room, and there on the chalkboard someone had written in big bold letters: "Gauthier got head tonight!" accompanied by a Polaroid picture of the victim's head. Ed got a kick out of it and smiled for the first time since I'd met him. I just shook my head and again asked, what have I gotten myself into?

The second week I got the chance to get back at Ed when I finally had the opportunity to drive; I was like a kid with my first car. I was driving the patrol car down a major street when I spotted my first stop. It was a Hell's Angel motorcycle gang member flying his colors and speeding down the highway. When I caught up to him and switched on my red lights, hitting the siren, I was astonished when he took off. So I did what any rookie would do—I chased him! The pursuit was on as we hit speeds of ninety to a hundred miles per hour. I thought Ed would be proud, but when I looked over at him all the color had gone from his face and he was staring blankly out the window. I think I might have shocked him, but when I finally got the motorcycle stopped Ed leaned over and began hitting me with his ticket book as he yelled, "Don't ever drive like that with me in the car again!"

"Okay," I said as I jumped out of the car and took my first bad guy into custody.

My next training officer was Danny, another senior officer who stood six feet six inches and had a great sense of humor. When we went to dinner, Danny would yell to the server, "Table for one and a half!" We must have been quite a sight, and Danny took advantage of that when we were patrolling the strip. While I was driving one night some tourists had stopped and were pointing at us, no doubt surprised to see a female officer. Danny, not wanting to miss an opportunity to be a wise guy, leaned over from the passenger seat and put his head in my lap. I punched him until he finally sat up, laughing hysterically. The people looked in shock, not knowing whether or not to laugh.

One night I asked Danny to stop at a gas station so I could go to the restroom, and he told me I had better be quick. I ran in and had to practically undress to use the bathroom, something the men couldn't relate to as this was not an issue for them.

When I emerged from the bathroom, to my surprise Danny was nowhere to be found. I was humiliated as I got on the portable radio and requested him to return. The radio mikes began clicking in response to my embarrassing situation. I got back at Danny, however, when we responded to a silent burglary alarm. Danny told me to cover the front as he went around to the back of the residence. Several minutes later, I heard the sound of the garage door closing, and I ran around the corner just in time to see Danny come sliding under the door just before it closed. He was covered in dirt and I was laughing so hard I almost wet my pants, promising him I wouldn't tell anyone, and he finally said, "Okay, we're even."

I got into my first fight as Danny's partner when we were dispatched to a riot that had broken out under the big tent at the carnival. When we arrived we saw a large group of drunken cowboys fighting and yelling obscenities as they taunted others to join in. Danny dashed into the crowd with me close behind as he began hitting the cowboys with his police baton. After hitting them, he would toss them over to me. I ordered each of them to the ground and handcuffed them using plastic flex cuffs. When it was all said and done, we had over a dozen men in custody and a crowd cheering us on. One drunken cowboy approached me to shake my hand, saying, "I've never seen a woman fight like that before."

Practical jokes were a way of dealing with the daily job stress and letting off some steam. One night when we did a pit stop, I challenged Danny to a race. I had gotten really fast and efficient at going to the bathroom, so I was not surprised when this time I arrived back at the patrol car before Danny. He just looked at me with a smirk on his face and asked, "Did you forget something?" He pointed to the back of my gun belt, where a stream of toilet paper dangled conspicuously. I was totally embarrassed and remembered walking through the casino, wondering why people were looking at me oddly.

Danny was amazingly funny and very skillful at interviewing witnesses and interrogating suspects. He made training a lot of fun and taught me the gift of laughing at myself, which was something I had never given myself permission to do. He rated me highly in many areas and approved me to go on to my next training officer.

In the third month of training the patrol commander requested that recruits who were ready to ride alone be released due to a shortage of officers. I was one of those released early and assigned to Main Station on swing shift. This station was known for its rough environment with many of the old-timers working there. My first night on patrol was interesting. When I walked into the station; the officers stopped everything and stared at me as one guy walked out of the locker room wearing only a towel around his waist. He was as shocked as I was as he retreated back into the locker room. I could already hear them saying, "What does this little woman think she's doing coming into our club?" As I dressed in the women's bathroom, I again thought, *Why didn't I go to law school?*

After changing into my uniform, I entered the smoke-filled briefing room crowded with male officers who sneered at me. I quickly found my seat at the back of the room. When I approached the briefing desk to get a hot sheet, the sergeant looked at me and said, "Rookie, I'd tell you a joke that would knock your tits off, but I see you've already heard it!" The men roared as the briefing room exploded in laughter. I could feel the blood rushing to my face as I was overwhelmed by embarrassment and humiliation. I walked back to my chair with my face flushed, my head down. I could not understand why these men were so dishonoring to my gender.

I was assigned to Sergeant Tom's squad; he had sat on my oral board when I hired on. He had recently been promoted and assigned to patrol after being a motorcycle officer for years. Sergeant Tom towered over me at six feet five inches, and he would become my gentle giant, someone I would befriend. Tom told me later he was so concerned about me working alone that he decided to put me in the outskirts of town in hopes I wouldn't get into any trouble. What Tom did not realize was that the bad guys from an adjacent jurisdiction would travel through my area to get home at night.

Tom's worst fear came true when I was out on patrol and rolled up on a robbery in progress. It was late in the shift, so most of my squad had gone back to the station, and the grave-yard officers were just getting out on the street. It was a transition time, so I would have no backup. It was 12:30 a.m. when I pulled into the convenience store parking lot. To my surprise, the clerk came running out, screaming, "They just robbed me!" He pointed to a large grey Oldsmobile with two young black males in it who were attempting to flee the scene when I drove up. I caught up to them at the red light and told the dispatcher that I had a possible robbery suspect vehicle, while I gave my location; just then the driver sped off through the red light! I immediately pursued—happy that I could spare Ed from the high-speed chase. I gave my locations to dispatch as I chased the suspects through another jurisdiction, when the lieutenant got on the radio insisting I tell him the nature of the pursuit. I did not have time to explain as I pursued the vehicle at speeds of ninety-five mph into oncoming traffic. As I chased the suspects into the housing projects, they spun the car out trying to make a turn. My last radio transmission, which would have given my location, was covered by the lieutenant's questions, "What's she got? Who's backing her?" so no one was able to hear my transmission and subsequently no one knew where I was…a dangerous situation to be sure.

As the suspect vehicle came to a stop, I came around the corner and hit my brakes as I slid within inches of the driver's door. I jumped out of my police car with my Remington shotgun, racking a round in the chamber as I pointed it at the two men still sitting in the car. This all happened in a few seconds, so I didn't have time to turn off my still-blaring siren. The noise awoke everyone, and it wasn't long before I was surrounded by a large crowd of angry black folks. I kept my focus on the suspects as the crowd closed in and began taunting me. They must have wondered what this little white female officer was doing all alone with no backup in sight. The siren's scream saved me as officers followed the sound to my location. I was relieved to see my backup arrive and the crowds begin to disperse. Sergeant Tom arrived shortly after as we loaded the last suspect into the vehicle. He smiled proudly at me and said, "Nice job, rookie!" When we got back to the station, the other officers gave me high fives, congratulating me on the arrest. I was on cloud nine as I soaked up the acceptance and affirmation of the men I worked with.

I worked my first three years on patrol at the Main Station, and about midpoint I changed squads and began to patrol in the area known as the Naked City. This was a very depressed area near downtown, predominantly apartment complexes that housed many of the Cuban refugees who had entered the country during President Carter's term in office. We discovered many of these Cubans were gang members operating in a culture very different from ours. Many of their apartments contained altars where the Cubans sacrificed animals to worship their gods.

Upon responding to a possible burglary in progress at one of these apartment buildings, I arrived to discover a rear window to a bedroom had been broken out. I didn't know if the suspect was still inside, so I waited for backup and called for a code red on the radio, which was for emergency traffic only. My backup officer and I crawled through the window and illuminated the inside with our flashlights. As we scoured the interior, we saw what looked like fish netting tacked to the walls and ceiling with fishhooks sewn into the corners of each square in the net. My partner accidentally scraped across the wall at one point and became entangled in the hooks. It reminded me of something from a bad horror film. I quickly cut him out, and we continued our search.

Behind the door of one room we were greeted with a macabre sight—a large dead bird hung upside down from the rafters with a spear through its body. It made me uneasy to imagine what we might find next. The last stop was the kitchen, where we found the refrigerator wrapped with a thick chain and secured by several padlocks. This was definitely one of the strangest things that I had ever seen. The suspect had obviously left the scene, and we cleared the channel by giving a code four, which meant that we were all right. The Crime Scene Analysts responded to the scene and processed it for any evidence left by the suspect. They also photographed the home's interior and cut the chains on the refrigerator to find out if there was a body inside. When the door was opened, we were hit with the stench and relieved to find it coming from rotten food and not a dead body.

One night as my shift ended I decided to check on Barry, an officer on my squad who had stopped a person in an alley behind some closed businesses. As I drove by, I saw his police car with the spotlight on a Cuban male standing in front of the car. I pulled in behind his patrol car with my lights off, and just as I approached them, the Cuban lunged at Barry, putting him in a headlock. They began to struggle. With my flashlight in my left hand I ran toward them as they fell over the curb. I saw Barry land on the ground as his pistol fell out of its holster onto the pavement. At that point, everything began to move in slow motion as the suspect reached for the gun. I was suddenly faced with a deadly force situation. I had to make a split-second decision whether to shoot the suspect and risk hitting Barry or to use the heavy flashlight I was carrying to take the suspect out. Using my momentum and a two-handed power swing, I struck the Cuban in the head just as he grabbed Barry's gun. I heard the sickening sound of a skull cracking as blood exploded from the wound, splattering all over Barry and me. The man fell in a clump beside Barry as I stepped on his hand, which was still gripping the gun. I thought for sure I had killed him. The adrenalin pumped through my body as I began to calm myself down.

Barry got up and pulled himself together as I called for an ambulance. The suspect lay motionless when my sergeant and detectives arrived, and we faced a possible homicide scene. I accompanied the suspect to the hospital, where, after several hours, the doctor announced he was stable and would probably survive. Upon his release from the hospital, he was shipped to Miami, where the Cuban refugees were detained prior to deportation.

My area, which was gang turf, was known for violent criminal activity. I became aware of a series of rapes involving a Cuban male who would stalk women as they got off work. This man would follow his victims to their apartments, and as they unlocked the door, he would shove them inside and violently beat and rape them.

One night as I patrolled my area during the time the suspect typically hit, my radio beeped, indicating a felony crime in progress. The dispatcher announced that the suspect had just hit again and was last seen running toward an alleyway to the rear of an apartment complex. I was close by, so I turned off my lights and drove quietly down an adjacent alley when I saw the silhouette of a man running toward me. I turned on my lights and accelerated toward the man, who I believed was the suspect. In the sudden illumination of my headlights, he stopped dead in his tracks. I slammed on my brakes, jumping out of the patrol car with my pistol pointing at him. He did not attempt to escape but put his hands in the air as I yelled for him to get on the ground. He yelled in his native language as I squeezed the slack out of my trigger and prepared to shoot him if he made any aggressive move.

Moments later a police helicopter arrived, flying overhead with its spotlight on us as I kept this man at gunpoint. I could hear the sirens as my backup responded. When I took the man into custody, another officer drove by with the victim in his vehicle. She told the officer that this was the man who had raped and beaten her. That night the crime series ended. Unfortunately, we would never go to court on this crime series. Justice was often avoided when the criminals were deported.

Although I had earned the respect of many male officers, there were still a few who made it no secret that they disliked me. I had an encounter with one of those officers when I stopped a sixteen-year-old boy who was driving a stolen vehicle. I had him in front of my patrol car in handcuffs as I gathered information on my radio when my backup arrived. I recognized the officer who worked on the black glove squad—named that because of their heavy-handedness. I watched in dread as he walked right past me and struck the boy in the face hard with his gloved fist.

"What do you think you're doing?" I yelled.

He just looked at me and said, "Teaching him a lesson. You got a problem with that, rookie?" The boy stared at me with fear in his eyes. His cheek began to swell, and he cried out in pain. I took hold of the boy and yelled at Gary, "You probably broke his cheekbone. Call an ambulance!" He gave me a dirty look and turned to walk away when I angrily yelled, "Since you laid hands on him, he's now yours! You transport him to juvenile hall!" Gary ignored me, so I called his sergeant and told him what had happened. He ordered me to transport the boy to the hospital. I would pay for this move; Gary promptly made it known that I was a snitch.

When dealing with suspects, I worked very differently than these men; I had to because of my gender and my physical limitations. I became proficient in surprising others, and my tactic was put to the test one night while on patrol. I had stopped a vehicle that had no license plates. I ordered the driver—a huge black man who stood about six feet four inches and weighed two hundred and forty pounds—out of the car. I noticed his arms were as big as my thighs, but I did not let his size intimidate me. I cautiously waited for his criminal history on the radio. The dispatcher finally responded, "Are you clear, 440?" which was a code indicating that the man was a wanted subject. I turned down the volume on my radio and listened as the dispatcher told me the man I had stopped was wanted for armed robbery and had a caution flag, meaning he would fight officers if arrested. I knew I couldn't show any fear. My best strategy would be the element of surprise. I very casually asked, "Do you mind if I check you for weapons? I get a little nervous out here by myself."

"No problem," he replied, whereupon I grabbed his thumbs and did a speed-cuffing technique on him. Before he could even blink he found himself in handcuffs.

"You're under arrest for an outstanding warrant for armed robbery," I stated. He just nodded as I led him to the passenger side of my vehicle and seat-belted him in. I wiped my sweaty palms on my pants as I walked around to the driver's side of my patrol car and got in. *He fights officers*, I kept thinking as I calmly spoke to him: "I have a question for you."

I was surprised when he respectfully replied, "Yes, ma'am."

"You have a history of fighting with police officers. Why didn't you fight me?"

I will never forget his reply: "Ma'am, this is the first time I've been to jail without a beating." It all suddenly made sense as I realized that many of the resisting arrests and battery on police officers were provoked by heavy-handed officers like Gary. I believe that in order to gain respect you have to show respect. That approach, I believe, kept me alive over the twenty-one years I worked as a police officer.

Although I tried my best to fit in with the guys, I was not comfortable with their patrol tactics, and they knew it. One night while targeting prostitutes in our area, the men on my squad told me they had obtained the telephone number of a pimp from one of the prostitutes they had arrested. They wanted me to call this man and tell him I was new in town and wanted to work for him. I agreed to their strategy and set up a meeting with the pimp in his hotel room. When I arrived, I approached the door in full uniform and knocked. A male voice responded, "Who is it?"

"Debbie," I said. When he opened the door stark naked, one of the male officers shoved me aside and immediately punched him in the face. The other officers jumped in, beating the guy mercilessly as they threw him facedown on the bed. I just stood there as one of the officers yelled, "Go ahead, get a shot in!"

"No, thanks, you guys have this covered," I said. "I'm clearing."

They yelled back, "Go ahead. We'll finish this up!" It was difficult trying to fit in with these guys. I was bothered by their brutal tactics, but I kept my mouth shut, not wanting to feed into their image of me as a snitch.

As one of just a few women police officers, I was a commodity when it came to undercover assignments. I had also become the police department's poster child, and my picture was being used throughout the city for recruitment purposes. One afternoon I received a telephone call from the commander of intelligence. He asked me if I would be interested in working undercover with their unit. I explained that my picture was posted on billboards all over town and that I would be at risk for being indentified. "Oh, don't worry about that," he said. "We will be disguising you." I told him I would ask my sergeant, and the commander replied, "I've already spoken to him. I'll see you tomorrow afternoon."

I reported to duty the next day as ordered and met Steve, a detective with whom I would be working undercover. Our first assignment was to apprehend a high-ranking member of a foreign drug cartel who had connections in Las Vegas. Steve took on the identity of a prominent businessman in the city, and I was his "girlfriend." We met the drug dealer and several of his bodyguards in a hotel room on the strip. I remember stepping into the room trying to suppress the growing anxiety of not knowing whether these people knew we were police officers; the fear of what could go wrong was intense. Two men searched us when we entered, and my attention was drawn to the pistols tucked in their waistbands. The main suspect sat on the bed with a pillow in front of him that I knew in my gut and would later discover was concealing a locked and cocked .45 caliber pistol pointed directly at us. Steve and the man talked for what seemed like a long time, and finally the transaction took place. Steve received a black briefcase containing a large quantity of cocaine. I stood there trying to appear calm but feeling the sweat running down the back of my legs. Steve, who had been working in the unit for several years, did his job calmly like a pro. We left the hotel without incident, carrying the evidence we needed to complete the warrant and serve it. A cover team watched the room as we obtained a signature from a judge. We returned later, along with our SWAT team, to serve the warrant. The drug dealer and his associates were placed under arrest, and the remainder of the cocaine and other drugs were seized.

I spent a hundred and twenty days temporarily assigned to this undercover unit and then had the option to return to patrol, which I gladly took. Shortly thereafter, my first sergeant, Tom, who had since been transferred to the SWAT team, called me one afternoon asking if I would like to be considered as a SWAT candidate. "We have one opening, and I believe you would be an asset to the team," he said. Tom was aware of my shooting skills and physical fitness, and believed I could handle the demands of the job. I was excited by this proposition since I admired and respected Tom for his leadership abilities, so I agreed to test for the position. Tom gave me some pointers, and I prepared for the test.

A week later I appeared for my oral board. I entered a room where Commander Tom sat, along with the team leader of the squad having the vacancy. I sat at the table across from them, introduced myself, and began answering their questions. Both Commander Tom and the team leader were hostile toward me, challenging each of my responses. I maintained my composure and confidently stuck to my answers. At the conclusion of the board, I was dismissed and told that I would be notified of my score. They would be selecting the top candidate from over a dozen applicants.

The next morning Sergeant Tom called me to say, "You came out number two, and I was really pulling for you in there." He added, "While I was defending you and challenging their concerns about having a woman on the SWAT team, the commander burst out and said, 'I'm not having any niggers or broads on my SWAT team!'" Tom said that that ended the discussion. He knew I would be disappointed, but he didn't want to subject me to an environment that was even more hostile toward women than patrol was.

Tom put my name in the hat to be considered for a new unit that the department was forming called SCAT, which stood for Street Crime Attack Team. I think the commander was concerned that I had heard about his comment regarding women and blacks, because he did a 180-degree turnaround and actually put in a good word for me, recommending me for this new unit. SCAT was created in 1983 and consisted of a team of officers who would employ decoy operations to reduce street crimes, such as purse snatches and robberies that were occurring in the downtown area and the strip. These areas were congested with tourists and had become a prime target for criminals.

The good news came just a few days later—I had been selected for the SCAT team. We would share office space with the SWAT team and would be working the swing shift with them as well. This was to be another undercover assignment in which my role would primarily be as decoy while the male officers on the team would cover me.

There were initially six of us on the team, and I worked along with Tim, who was also a decoy officer. Tim often disguised himself as drunk or wheelchair-bound with money protruding from one of his pockets. One night some of the guys made a bet with Tim, which he lost, so he had to dress up as a woman and be the decoy that night. Tim actually looked really good; I was a little jealous! He started to like wearing nylons and high heels too. I don't think Tim's wife was as amused by it as we were. I think Tim used to steal his wife's nylons, which really made her mad. I would be the other decoy, posing as a pregnant woman or a senior citizen carrying a purse with money exposed from a pocket. Professional makeup artists helped us with our disguises, and we were surprised by the success of our operations.

One night I was seated on a bench at a downtown street corner, waiting for the bus to arrive. I noticed two white men standing behind me, looking very nervous. They paced up and down the sidewalk as my cover team watched them closely. The closest officer, Danny (my former training officer), was across the street wearing a maintenance uniform, posed as part of the cleaning crew. The other officers were stationed at various locations around me; I wore a body wire so I could communicate with any of them in case of an emergency.

I sat on the bench in my pregnant woman disguise, clutching my purse with a hundred dollar bill sticking out a side pocket. The two men had spotted the money and were waiting for the opportunity to strike when a large truck drove by, blocking Danny's view. The taller man lunged at me and grabbed my purse. I began to scream as he jerked the purse from my grip. Both suspects ran northbound on Third toward Fremont Street. As they approached the corner, a group of men who were picketing at the Golden Nugget Hotel heard my screams and spotted the two men running away with my purse. These citizens tackled the suspects and began to beat them before we arrived. As I ran up holding my padded stomach, one of the men politely said, "Ma'am, here's your purse that was stolen." They were amazed when I showed them my police badge. I thanked them for their assistance. The two suspects, now bleeding from their beating, were handcuffed and transported to jail.

We averaged two felony arrests per shift, but were often slowed down because Danny loved a fight and enjoyed breaking noses, so we often had to take suspects to the hospital before jail. In those days, internal affairs complaints were rare and a beating was considered part of the street justice. I enjoyed the excitement and dynamic nature of this work but grew tired of the routine at the end of our shift, which included a debriefing at the local bar. The officers typically would become intoxicated and obnoxious, and I was often the brunt of sexual jokes. They pressured me to be a part of their activities, which didn't sit well with me. After being forced to drive in the undercover police vehicle with my drunken sergeant one night, I knew it was time to transfer back to patrol.

Once back in patrol, I noticed an announcement for the position of field training officer, which appealed to me because this role would prepare me to test for sergeant when I was eligible. I tested for the position and was one of two females selected. I transferred to the Southeast Area Command working swing shift.

When I arrived for my new assignment briefing, the other training officers were cold toward me as I continued to wear the label of "snitch." I discovered that once an officer is labeled, it is almost impossible to shed that reputation. I often lunched alone when we did not have recruits riding with us because the officers did not want to associate with me.

During one of our breaks from training I was on patrol and spotted a driver swerving in the lane ahead of me. I figured he was drunk, so I stopped him. I asked the driver, a tall, lean cowboy in jeans and a flannel shirt, to step out of his truck when I noticed he had difficulty walking and his speech was slurred. I conducted a series of field sobriety tests, and the cowboy failed every one. I placed him under arrest for driving while under the influence of alcohol. He became extremely upset at this point and pleaded, "Ma'am, please take me home. I can't go to jail." I told him it was just a misdemeanor crime and he would probably be out of jail before I finished my paperwork. He continued to beg me, "Officer, please, I can't go to jail!"

Finally I said, "Why not?"

"You promise not to laugh?"

"Sure," I replied.

"I'm wearing my wife's underwear."

I did not keep my promise. I broke out in hysterical laughter.

"You promised not to laugh," he said. I apologized and asked him why he was wearing his wife's underwear. "It's something I like to do when I drink." I shook my head in disbelief and took him to jail, where he was turned over to the corrections officer to be strip-searched. I really felt bad for the guy when the officer came out of the room waving a frilly pair of women's lacey red underwear as he pushed my prisoner into the holding cell.

You see pretty much everything when you are in patrol and, for better or worse, become desensitized after a while. One such call occurred one afternoon when I met the mother of a four-teen-year-old boy who told me that her son had been selling magazines and was sexually assaulted by a woman in an apart-ment. Something about her story did not sound right to me, but I took a statement anyway and went to the apartment to investigate.

I knocked at the door, and a large Russian-looking woman answered, inviting me inside. I advised her that she was the sus-pect in an alleged sexual assault and was reading the Miranda rights when I noticed a stain on the carpet where the boy said the assault had occurred. I requested that the crime scene ana-lysts process the scene, and the woman finally confessed to hav-ing sex with the boy. I advised her that she was under arrest for statutory sexual seduction and transported her to jail.

My instincts still felt like something was "off," and I just knew there was something the boy wasn't telling me. I soon found out what that missing information was during the wom-an's strip search. After removing her blouse and bra, she said, "Officer, I have something to tell you." She proceeded to inform me that she was in the process of a sex change and that she was still a male on the lower part of her body. It took me a minute to process that information. After a moment I told her to put her blouse back on, and I went to get a male corrections officer to complete the strip search of the lower half of my prisoner.

It now all made sense why the boy was afraid to tell me what really had happened. I informed the sexual assault detectives who were doing the follow-up investigation and learned that this man had indeed raped the boy. My heart went out to the young boy, who would be permanently scarred from this event. I was never subpoenaed to court, so the case was probably plea-

Debra Gauthier

bargained, sparing the boy from having to share his testimony in a courtroom.

As a patrol officer, I also faced the realities of death. One night I responded to the dreaded "suspicious odor" call in an apartment complex. I could already smell the noxious stench that was coming from an upstairs apartment. I found the apartment it was coming from locked up and dark inside. I got the key from the manager, who told me the tenant lived there alone and had not been seen in almost a week. With apartment key in hand, I headed back upstairs. Before entering the apartment I packed my nostrils with Vicks to block the odor. I unlocked the door and held my breath as I entered the apartment, relying on my flashlight for light because the power had been turned off.

It was a balmy August evening, and the inside of the apartment was like a sauna. With sweat running down my face, I peered into the bathroom and saw a large object draped over the tub. I realized I was looking at the rear end of the man who lived in the apartment. From the looks of things, he had apparently died on the toilet and fallen into the tub. He was now so bloated that his form was almost unrecognizable as a body. The skin had rotted black, and when I saw maggots crawling on him I bolted out of the apartment, fighting back the urge to vomit. Soon the coroner showed up. Two men unloaded a gurney and plastic body bag. They told me later that the body had fallen apart when they tried to remove it and they had to place the pieces into the bag. I told them, "Thanks for sharing!" as I again attempted to hold back the urge to vomit. I drove to the station, where I showered and changed—anything to get the smell off of me.

I would face many life-and-death situations throughout my career. On one particular night I responded to a call at a business complex where a man was seen entering an office carrying a gun. It was about 9:30 p.m. as I pulled into the complex and shut off my lights. As I entered a courtyard, the maintenance man approached. He led me to the office in question, informing me he was the one who had witnessed the gun-wielding man. I told him to wait in the parking lot for my backup and then show them where I was when they arrived.

With my gun out, I walked down a long empty hallway in the direction of the real estate office where the man with the gun allegedly was. I stayed close to the wall, and when I was a few feet from the office door I heard footsteps at the end of the hallway. Just then I looked up to see the suspect come around the corner with a locked and cocked .45 caliber pistol pointed at the hostage's head. When he saw me, the hostage's eyes got big and he made a brash decision: with no warning he broke away from the suspect and ran toward me. With my gun trained on the suspect, my heart pounded as I waited for the hostage to move out of the kill zone. I now found myself looking down the barrel of the suspect's weapon. The entire incident happened in only a few quick seconds, and before I could shoot, the suspect retreated back around the corner and into the real estate office, where he then barricaded himself.

"What were you thinking?" I yelled at the hostage. In my head I was thinking that move could have gotten us both killed. I told him to wait at my patrol car, and I immediately called for a code red, which meant emergency traffic only, advising the dispatcher what had happened and requesting the SWAT team. I advised my backup officer to set up a perimeter as I maintained my position. A few moments later I could hear the sirens coming, and I began a dialogue with the suspect through the door. I told him to come out so we could resolve the situation. "I'm not going anywhere," he responded. "If you try and come in, I will kill you and myself!"

I was at a standstill when the SWAT team and negotiators arrived and took over my position. It was a relief to get off the hard floor I had been kneeling on for over an hour. A few

Debra Gauthier

minutes later the SWAT officers deployed gas and ordered the man out; he finally surrendered and was taken into custody. I transported the suspect to jail, and he told me that the owner of the real estate office (his hostage) had cheated him out of a large sum of money and he had planned to kill him and dump his body in the desert. As I replayed the incident in my head, I realized that the action of the hostage bolting from the suspect actually had saved me from getting in a shootout in that hallway.

I had another narrow escape after responding to a family disturbance call. As I left the scene and got into my patrol car, which was parked on the dirt shoulder of the road, I noticed headlights coming toward me at a high rate of speed. I had a few seconds to decide whether to stay in my vehicle, and I knew at that moment my best chance to survive would be to get away from the lights. I jumped out of the driver's side and pressed against a chicken wire fence that surrounded the property, when all of a sudden the headlights were on me and a grey primer pickup truck, swerving to avoid hitting my patrol car head-on, was now coming straight at me. Kenny, my partner who had been on the call with me, was still standing with the couple on their porch and yelled, "Deb, look out!" The driver suddenly turned his truck in between me and my patrol car, ripping the car door off its hinges as he sped by me. I quickly turned my head aside and used my arm to block my face from the results of the impact as the truck's side view mirror violently struck my left forearm, almost pulling me down the street.

I immediately jumped into my police car and turned it around to pursue the suspect as I screamed on the radio, "Control, I'm in pursuit of a GMC pickup truck, primer gray in color, that just struck my vehicle and almost ran me over!" Without my car door, the noise of the wind and siren were making my radio transmission unintelligible until Kenny joined the pursuit and communicated the details of the events to the dispatcher. I was able to close in on the suspect vehicle as I approached speeds of over ninety mph, but I was unable to read the license plate. The suspect suddenly turned off his headlights, driving into the desert, where I stopped until my backup arrived. At this point the police helicopter appeared on the scene and began to search for the suspect vehicle in the desert area just ahead of me. I realized I was now trembling from shock as the reality of what I had just experienced began to set in.

Once we established a perimeter, the helicopter spotted the truck, which had careened into a ditch; the driver was found hiding under a bush. The air unit guided police officers into the area on foot, where they took the suspect into custody. An officer drove up to me a short time later and asked, "Is this the guy that tried to run you over?"

I looked into the front seat and saw a man covered in blood and mud, and I replied, "I didn't get a chance to see his face, but this has got to be him." The officer transported him to jail and discovered that the suspect was not only driving under the influence of alcohol and drugs but had stolen the truck and had been recently paroled from prison.

My sergeant responded to the location, and an ambulance was called to transport me to the hospital. I refused to go in the ambulance, so my sergeant ordered me into his patrol car and transported me himself. The guy drove like a maniac, and I realized that I should have accepted the ambulance ride because I was surely going to die. By some miracle we arrived at the hospital safely, where the emergency room doctor told me I had damaged the ligaments in my forearm. He put me in a splint, gave me a tetanus shot, and sent me home.

That night I was so pumped up with adrenalin that I had difficulty falling asleep; when I did finally doze off the ringing of the phone woke me up. To my surprise, it was the sheriff calling. He told me that he was proud of me for doing a good job and asked how I was feeling. Sheriff Moran was an "old school" cop, and I had evidently earned his respect. Before hanging up he said, "I admire your tenacity and courage, Officer. Keep up the good work!" I sat there savoring the moment as I let this man's affirmation sink deep into my soul, healing some of the wounds that I had suffered from other men.

While working as a field training officer, I was transferred to the west side of town—an area known as predominantly black and also for its violence to officers. It was a small area but very densely populated, containing several housing projects that were controlled by local gangs. Because of the danger of working this area, we were assigned to two-man units. I would be working with a training officer named Larry, who had transferred from Detroit and was accustomed to working in this type of setting. Larry was very laid-back and easygoing, which made his street smarts even more unassuming. He typically carried a knife in his pocket that he would discreetly pull out when interrogating suspects, menacingly placing the blade against their throat for its intimidation factor. It was very effective, and Larry was able to get the information he needed.

Larry helped me get acquainted with my new area by introducing me to the fellows in the projects. I would need to establish my reputation before I could successfully work this area with a new recruit. One afternoon as we drove into the projects, we noticed a group of gang members standing against a wall. The men looked at us with hate-filled eyes as they spit on the ground in a display of disrespect. As we walked toward them, Larry pointed out the gang leader to me, a six-foot-two black male who was standing in the center of the group. Larry said, "I've got your back. Go introduce yourself." I noticed Larry had his gun out and was holding it against his leg. I followed suit and took the mace out of my belt, hiding it against my leg as I walked up to these men. I asked the leader what his name was, and he ignored me, spitting on the ground by my feet. The other men all laughed. I asked him again what his name was, and he just stood there as I told him he was under arrest for loitering. They were all still laughing as I sprang into action. I sprayed mace into the gang leader's face while sweeping his feet out from under him. He hit the ground hard, and I drove my knee into the back of his neck. I quickly handcuffed him as he barraged me with obscenities.

The other gang members kept their distance as we loaded the ring leader into our patrol car and sped off. While en route to the station, the suspect continued to threaten me, saying, "I'm going to kill you when I see you again." I did not realize it, but Larry shrewdly had keyed the radio mike inside the police car so the suspect's remarks were recorded on tape. That recording provided us with the evidence to officially charge him with threatening a police officer. At the parole hearing, the judge revoked his parole and sent him back to prison based on the tape recording.

After that incident, the word out on the street was that there was this crazy white female officer who knew karate and she was not to be messed with. I was glad that Larry had taken the time to make the introduction to the players in my area. I am certain that it saved my life.

The next academy class graduated, and we received a group of new recruits. I was assigned a female officer named Christie who was five feet eight inches and weighed one hundred and sixty pounds. She looked like she could handle herself in a fight, and I was glad to have her as my partner. It wasn't long before Christie had an opportunity to prove herself when we responded to a call of a man high on PCP who was breaking the windows out of his house. When we pulled up, we saw a black male lifting a metal trash can over his head and screaming at the top of his lungs. In the past I had encountered other people under the influence of this particular drug. It caused them to be extremely dangerous with almost superhuman strength. I told Christie to grab her baton and distract him while I came around behind him. When she approached, the suspect launched the trash can to the other side of the yard, yelling, "What are you going to do about it?" Christie kept his attention as I ran up behind him and jumped on his back, putting him in a chokehold and squeezing until he fell unconscious. Christie grabbed him and immediately put the handcuffs on, and we carried his bulky unconscious body to the patrol car, loading him into the back seat. When he awoke, he began violently screaming and kicking the seat and window with his feet, trying to break out of the car. Even though he was in restraints, he made quite a commotion. I pulled Christie aside and coated the suspect with mace as he choked and continued to fight. We rode to jail code five, signifying our combative prisoner, and the jailers met us outside the facility.

Many nights were spent in foot pursuits chasing suspects involved in drug transactions. This was common in our area, and we got very good at working together. When Christie and I drove up on a drug buy, the dealer would see us, and the chase was on—I would jump out of the patrol vehicle while my partner radioed our location and direction of travel. I chased suspects over fences and through yards while my partner would parallel my foot pursuit in the vehicle, waiting for the suspect so we could then close in and take custody.

One night while on foot patrol, we encountered two women fighting; one had pulled a knife and was about to stab the other as we ran up. I struck her with my baton, and she dropped the knife, screaming, "You broke my arm!" That was enough to draw a large hostile crowd around Christie and me as we stood back to back, me holding on to the prisoner. We had our guns out and told the crowd if they did not disperse we would shoot them. Our bluff worked, and they began to move so that we could get to our police car. Once we were in the vehicle, they began throwing bottles and closed in on us. I pressed on the accelerator and sped out just in time.

I was grateful that I had studied martial arts for several years after graduating from the academy. I had been on the force for almost four years, and new classes were graduating every six months. That training came in handy when I walked into a bar one night on a disturbance call and observed a crowd of people that had been fighting. When I ordered two of the patrons outside, a belligerent black female who easily weighed a hundred and seventy pounds menacingly smashed her drinking glass against the side of the bar and threatened to cut me with the broken glass. In one motion, I grabbed her wrist, pulled her backward off the barstool, and dragged her out of the bar kicking and screaming.

One of the worst fights I ever got into was with another big violent black woman who had escaped from a mental institution. When I approached her, she caught me off guard and punched me in the mouth, putting my metal braces through my lower lip. I cringed in pain and drew my baton, striking her in the face with a power swing. This woman didn't even flinch. She responded by kicking me hard in the chest, which sent me flying backward over a table. I knew the fight was on, and I was concerned about her getting hold of my gun. So instead of wrestling with her, I quickly got her into a choke hold and squeezed until she was unconscious. That ended the fight pretty quickly. It was quite a sight when I arrived at jail, both the suspect and I thoroughly bloody and beat up. The corrections officer sarcastically asked, "Who won the fight?" The suspect had a swollen cheek and eye caused by the blow from my baton. I had blood down the front of my uniform; my braces were still stuck to the bottom of my lip. Later at the hospital, the doctor removed the metal from my lip and stitched up the hole.

Days later I ran into this same woman when she was picking up trash in an alleyway. There were now warrants out on her. This time I was extremely cautious in my approach, and, to my surprise, she was as docile as a lamb. I arrested her without incident. I knew she did not remember me. I, however, would never forget her.

Dishonor and Grace

> It is sown in dishonor; it is raised in glory; it is sown in weakness; it is raised in power.
>
> 1 Corinthians 15:43 (NIV)

It was not long into my career when I began to endure sexual harassment from several officers. One particular officer, Pat, gave me a lot of trouble. He was a big guy, about six feet three inches, and weighed around two hundred pounds. He would always block my way as I tried to exit the briefing room at the end of the shift. He enjoyed making inappropriate comments about my physique, and the other officers would laugh and encourage him. Pat followed me around on calls at night and had become a real nuisance to me. I repeatedly told him to leave me alone—to no avail.

One night the lieutenant saw Pat pressing against me in the hallway, and I was ordered to prepare a written statement detailing all of the incidents of sexual harassment. I said, "Lieutenant, with all due respect, I have to work with these guys. If I comply with your order, they will blackball me and make my job miserable." The lieutenant told me that he understood how I felt but that this officer had been a problem for many years and he needed to be dealt with. I had no choice at that point but to follow his order.

When I returned to work after my regular days off, I found a dildo hanging on my locker with my name etched in it. That was only the beginning of my nightmare. Every time I walked into the briefing room, the officers took the opportunity to bump into me and give me the silent treatment the entire shift. When I went out to my patrol car to log on the radio, officers keyed their mikes and covered my transmission—meaning they purposefully blocked me from radioing in to the station. This put me in great danger when I was out on the street because nobody knew my location. About midway through the shift one night, Mel, a black male officer, met me on a call and told me the other patrol officers would beat up anyone caught talking to me. He said, "You're on your own out here...watch your back." I could not believe what he was telling me. Tension increased as the night went on, and I feared I would have no backup from my fellow officers should something happen.

Sure enough, I responded to a fight call later that night. When I discovered I indeed had no backup, I finally called my sergeant. He pulled up in his patrol car, saying, "What's up?" as if he didn't know what was going on. I said to him, "I told the lieutenant I did not want to be part of his complaint against Pat because I would end up out here working alone, and now I am."

He replied, "So?"

I just laughed at his complacent attitude and said, "Sir, I'm going home because this is your problem, not mine!"

"Suit yourself," he said. I went home and cried myself to sleep that night. I could not believe the way I was being treated by my fellow officers. It hurt me deeply.

I stayed home the rest of the week and did some serious soul searching. I had typed up a letter of resignation, believing that this was a good time to get out of law enforcement and go on to law school. Nancy, my sorority sister in college, had gone on to law school when we graduated. I went on to join the police department. We were talking one night, and she asked me why I wanted to subject myself to the kind of treatment I would get working with the "good old boys." She said, "Deb, you've got your college degree. Why don't you go to law school?" I realized then that this was still where I wanted to be.

I told her, "Because this is where I want to make a difference." I really did enjoy the challenge of the job and being on the front line of the judicial system. I was only now becoming truly aware of the cost.

Pat continued his harassment against me. One night as I leaned over to pick up my radio, he came up behind me and pressed against me in a sexually provocative manner while the lieutenant on duty watched. Later that night, the lieutenant called me into his office. He placed in front of me a complaint against Officer Pat. I informed him I did not want to sign anything because I had to work with these men and rely on them for backup. The lieutenant would not accept my refusal and ordered me to sign the complaint. He then initiated an investigation that resulted in the officer's suspension, and from that day forward I experienced the backlash. At the station, I was shunned by the male officers. When I tried to log onto the radio in my police car, the male officers keyed their mikes so I could not talk. I was dispatched to dangerous calls without any backup, just as I'd expected would happen.

I began receiving threats on my life and was told by a couple of my male friends on the force that I was on my own and that if anyone helped me, they would be "dealt with." This had a chilling affect on me, hindering me from performing my job well. I met with Sergeant Tom to request that he correct the situation. As I drove home that night in tears, I reminded myself again that quitting was not an option.

As a result of that incident, I was transferred to another station, where I had to earn the respect of my fellow officers all over again. I felt almost hopeless and fought back the fear as I prepared to face a new group of officers. Any trust I had hoped to build with these men was destroyed by the incident with the lieutenant; many of the men hated me before I ever crossed their path. I did my job under very emotionally and mentally harsh conditions, not realizing how much stress I was under until I went to the dentist for my checkup. He asked me if I had been eating rocks for breakfast because I had grinded my molars flat from clenching my teeth.

In July 1986 I was promoted to sergeant after scoring high on the written exam and oral board. As the first female officer hired under the same standards as the men, this was a tremendous achievement because I had been promoted based on my performance, not my minority status. After only five years, all the hard work and perseverance had paid off. I was very excited and now glad that I had not quit. My first assignment as a sergeant was the Northwest Area Command on the graveyard shift, working with a group of renegade officers. I began my tour of duty at ten p.m. and ended at eight a.m., which turned my world upside down. I had difficulty readjusting on my days off and usually missed a night of sleep in the transition. I met with the prior sergeant, who was retiring, and he shared a little bit of information on each one of the guys who would be working for me. He warned me about the two senior officers on the squad, Kurt and Bill. He informed me that Bill had a drinking problem and often showed up to work drunk. He said, "If Bill shows up with a Big Gulp full of water, you can bet he's been drinking all day." I was amazed by this and asked the sergeant why he had not dealt with the matter. He replied, "Rookie, these guys are about ready to retire. Why go there?" He assured me that Kurt would babysit Bill on those nights, driving around with him in his police car while Bill slept it off.

The first night on my new assignment I walked into the briefing room wearing my shiny new sergeant's stripes as I spotted Bill and his Big Gulp on the desk in front of him. As I walked up to hand him the briefing sheet and introduce myself, I was almost knocked over by the alcohol smell on his breath. At the end of the briefing, I called out to Bill, "Meet me in my office." The other guys on the squad all groaned and taunted Bill as he swaggered down the hall to meet with me. As he entered my office, I closed the door behind him and said, "Have a seat." I was doing my best not to appear nervous as I counseled a man who was old enough to be my dad. I began the conversation very casually: "So, Bill, what is your goal this year?"

He looked at me dumbfounded and replied, "To retire."

"You're not going to make that one. What's your next goal?"

His eyes got big, and he sat up in his chair. "What do you mean by that?"

I pulled out his file and placed in front of him the pattern of excessive absences over the past year. "Your behavior," I said, "is unacceptable, and you have got to make a decision tonight about your future." I told him that this would be the last time he showed up to work intoxicated. "We can go the progressive disciplinary route," I said, "and you will be out of a job in about three months at the rate you are going."

Bill looked at me like a child who'd been harshly scolded and replied with much heaviness, "Yes, ma'am."

My heart began softening toward him, and I ended up driving him home after he agreed to take time off work to attend an alcohol rehabilitation center and dry out. I told him I would be writing him up for violating policy this night and would withhold issuing any discipline until he successfully completed the program and kept himself clean for the following year. He gratefully thanked me and said, "I'll see you in six weeks, Sarge, and I will be a new man."

"Let's hope so, for everyone's sake," I replied.

It wasn't long before I was faced with my next challenge when the dispatcher called, complaining that one of my officers had logged on the radio with a foreign accent, trying to be funny. The officer had been getting away with this for months and the dispatcher thought she would find out what the rookie sergeant was all about. A short time later I heard an officer with a Norwegian accent stop a vehicle. I thought this could be none other than Kurt, so I headed to his location. I stood off to the side watching him interview the driver and write a citation. When he was finished, I said, "How about a cup of coffee?"

He looked at me with suspicion and replied, "Why not?"

After ordering our drinks, I began a casual conversation with Kurt. I told him I was relying on him as my senior man. "Kurt," I said, "I'm going to be starting a pilot program involving a TDY [temporary duty assignment] with dispatch, and I am going to have you lead it off."

He looked shocked and replied, "Those women down there will kill me."

I nodded in agreement. "I know."

He leaned back in his chair and, grinning, replied, "I got your message, Sarge. I'll knock off the nonsense on the radio." He shook my hand in agreement and paid for my tea. I started to think that I might like this sergeant business.

I had a very diverse squad. At one end were my two senior officers who had about sixty years of law enforcement between them, and on the other end were two rookie officers with about one year total between the two of them. My rookies were a lot of fun and reminded me of my training days and zeal as a new officer. Liability was the last thing on their mind. I would get calls from them on the radio asking things like, "Hey, Sarge, we've got this guy barricaded in an apartment…okay if we kick the door in?"

"What's the charge?" I asked.

There was a long pause on the radio and then they said, "He ran from us; we're not sure until we get inside and talk to him."

I laughed and said, "Another night, guys; let that one go."

I could hear the disappointment in their voices as they replied, "Copy that, Sarge."

Debra Gauthier

I gained a lot of experience as a supervisor and was glad I was being forced to learn to overcome some serious challenges. One of those was the hours we worked. One early morning at about 4:30, I went home for lunch and was so exhausted I fell asleep. I didn't know how long I had slept when I jumped up off the couch and was shocked to see the clock said 7:00 a.m. I had set the alarm, but I was so tired I didn't hear it. I splashed water on my face and raced back to the station just in time for debriefing. Most of my officers were already in the briefing room, and I must have looked pretty bad because one of them said, "Bad night, Sarge?" I grumbled as I signed off their reports and dismissed them. When I got into the locker room, I looked in the mirror and almost fainted. I had dark circles under my eyes and a large pillow crease on the left side of my cheek. No wonder my guys were chuckling when they made that comment.

I had spent less than a year on this squad when I saw the announcement for the academy training sergeant position. My heart was in training because of what I had to endure being the pioneer and paving the way for other women. I knew that it was important to reach a hand back to those that would follow in my footsteps. As a role model I would have the opportunity to share what I had learned as a field training officer and to help others succeed. I had grown close to these guys and did not want to leave them. Bill had returned to work, sober for the first time in years, and he even stopped and arrested a DUI. There were tears in his eyes when I told the squad that I would be transferring to the academy. They said, "We understand, Sarge. A woman's got to do what a woman's got to do! We're going to miss you."

The last night of briefing I walked in and sat down at the front table. As I looked out across the room, I noticed all my guys had their heads down on the table. I thought, *What the heck is going on here?* When I began to conduct briefing, the guys all lifted their heads, and each was wearing a Groucho Marx nose with glasses and mustache attached. It was the funniest thing I'd ever seen, and I burst out laughing. They said their good-byes, and we shared cake together as they wished me farewell. I was truly touched by their respect and compassion. Before Bill went out on the street that night, he said, "Sarge, you were the first supervisor to ever call me on my stuff." He extended his hand. "Thanks."

I choked back the tears as I took his hand and warmly said, "It has been an honor working with you." It had taken a lot of courage for Bill to face his drinking problem and make a change, and I told him I was very proud of him.

I left that squad to become the first woman on the academy staff and would be in charge of the staff as well as training ninety police recruits. When I arrived at the academy, I found that the officers there had "prepared my welcome." As I began unloading my things, I pulled open my desk drawer and suddenly fell backwards as a loud boom rang out. I looked under the desk, and found a wire going from the drawer to the trigger on a revolver that was taped underneath and pointing at me. This did not amuse me, so I walked down the hall into the staff office, where the guys were holding back their laughter. I said, "Very funny, guys. Let's get back to work."

It would not be long before I became frustrated in my new assignment because the lieutenant was undermining my authority with the men. He burdened me with many of his administrative tasks while he went off with the boys and played with the recruits in the academy. One of the lieutenant's favorite tricks was to go into the classroom just before lunch and take the recruits' lunches and eat them. He had a big slingshot that he would set up in the parking lot launching the oranges and apples that he had gathered from the lunch boxes.

I finally settled into the new position and looked forward to graduating our first academy class. We began with ninety police recruits and graduated fifty-six. I earned a lot of respect from the recruits and the staff as I stood up under the tremendous amount of pressure of being a female academy officer. I will never forget the first inspection of the academy class. I marched out with my staff and the lieutenant, and we began our inspection of the new recruits. They shook and stumbled through their definitions and codes as we yelled at them. I took the quiet approach, which caught them off guard; many of these guys buckled under the pressure. I approached one recruit and said, "Give me the definition for a crime, Recruit," while I snatched his gun from his hand and ran my white glove over it.

He loudly replied, "Mom, a crime is a ..." He stopped.

"What did you call me, Recruit?" I yelled.

"Mom, I mean, ma'am!" he said. The poor guy just got more flustered as I continued to challenge him on his response. He unfortunately did not make it through the first week of the academy before he quit.

I had a lot of fun with the recruits and got to know many of them during the classes I taught in report writing, criminal procedures, and civil service rules. I juggled my teaching duties with running the academy staff office and performing the other tasks associated with a sergeant's position. Unlike the sergeant in my academy, I would suit up and go on the runs with the guys in the afternoon, and I made it a point to be actively involved in their training. This kept me abreast of the class's progress and my staff's performance. Once I had the unpleasant task of disciplining one of my training officers for screaming ethnic slurs at an Asian recruit in front of the entire class. He did not take the discipline well and created a lot of animosity between me and the other staff members.

The lieutenant who had been actively involved in the training was busy overseeing the building of the new academy facility and his own personal home at the same time. He was later investigated for allegedly using some of the supplies from the academy on his custom home.

One afternoon my staff and I had the recruits practicing at the firearms range, which was located on the side of a mountain, when we heard an explosion in the valley below us. I immediately got on the radio and said, "Control, this is the academy sergeant. What is the nature of that explosion?" She told me to stand by, and I continued to watch as a large cloud of bluish brown smoke headed in our direction. I didn't know if this was a chemical explosion, but judging by the color in the smoke, I knew it was toxic. I didn't wait for a reply from the dispatcher but yelled to the recruits and staff, "Everyone, up to the range house!" I ordered everyone inside.

As we secured the windows and doors, shutting off all vents leading to the outside, the cloud descended on us like a heavy fog. I got a telephone call from my lieutenant, informing me that a rocket fuel plant had exploded and the cloud of smoke was indeed highly toxic. They did not know the number of casualties, but the explosion had leveled a marshmallow plant located next to it. This was my first time handling a major disaster as a police sergeant. I appreciated the lieutenant's help. He said, "Have the recruits dress in their formal uniforms and caravan out to the command post, ASAP!" Before he hung up he told me he was counting on me to get everyone there safely and in order.

A flurry of activity ensued after I instructed the academy staff to prepare the recruits and inform them we would be leaving in fifteen minutes. We loaded five police cars with recruits while several others drove their personal vehicles as we formed a caravan, responding to the disaster area with red lights and sirens blasting. Traffic on the freeway was gridlocked, so we drove in the emergency lane until we got close to the area.

We finally arrived at the command post, which was set up at local park approximately five miles from the disaster site; the fire department was responsible for the inner perimeter and set up their command post at the site. They were properly equipped with gas masks, unlike our officers, who were subjected to breathing toxic fumes for many hours. I quickly made up a roster and organized the recruits into small teams responsible for a variety of duties in the command post and out on the perimeter directing traffic. It was one of the most challenging situations I have ever faced, and I felt the pressure of having to trust a new recruit with police responsibility under high stress conditions.

We set up a staging area for parents and school officials to deal with the evacuation of nearby schools. Parents were frantic as they waited to find out if their children were alive. In spite of the major devastation to property, there were few casualties, as most of the employees from both plants had some prior warning, giving them time to escape from the area. The explosion started with a fire in one of the gas lines, causing the rocket fuel tank explosion. A supervisor in the plant had spotted the fire at the early stages, and he immediately evacuated the plant. If it had not been for the quick action of this man, hundreds of people would have lost their lives.

As a result of my performance at the disaster scene, I was nominated for an award given by the city manager's office for recognition of outstanding contributions and excellence in public service. I had worked through the challenge of being the first woman on the academy staff and received respect and admiration from the recruits—that is, until a situation occurred over which I had no control. On the first day of the second academy class, I was conducting inspections with the other officers when I saw leather gear and a gun go flying over the fence. I looked to see who had thrown the equipment and realized it was thrown by my commanding officer.

This incident became the catalyst to remove the commander from the academy. He was replaced by another lieutenant who had his own private agenda, which included replacing me with a sergeant of his choosing. He told me I would be training my replacement and moving over to in-service training. I asked to remain on the academy side of the training and explained that I was not interested in the other position. He responded, "That's my decision. If you don't like it you can leave."

I knew it was time to leave, and I was recruited for a sergeant's position in the Detective Bureau. I was selected and assigned to the economic crimes section in charge of the fraud detail. When I arrived on the first day, I entered a large office with six detectives sitting at their desks facing each other. My desk was on the far wall facing the other detectives and there were no cubicle walls, so it was very noisy and distracting. When I walked in they all stopped what they were doing and stared at me. One of the senior white-haired officers asked, "Who are you?"

I replied, "I'm the sergeant. Who are you?"

The man smirked and said, "We're the fraud squad." I thought, *This is going to be interesting, supervising officers who are old enough to be my dad!* They weren't very friendly and considered me more of a nuisance than a threat. When I returned from lunch the first day, one of the detectives had added up their badge numbers and the total was still lower than mine. They had made their point that I was the rookie on the squad!

I began to sense the arrogant attitudes and passive resistance to complying with orders. I knew I would have to take a different approach than I took while supervising the academy personnel. It was a culture shock to go from such a structured environment working with inexperienced officers to a very informal, unstructured environment with experienced men. I asked the senior detective to instruct me in white-collar investigations and told him I would be his trainee, and he liked that. I began to develop a rapport with the squad and was able to get them motivated to do their jobs again. I accomplished that by working several white-collar sting operations with the Federal Bureau of Investigations targeting telemarketers. I had a long way to go to get these detectives up from their desks and out in the field. They had to find their guns on their messy desks, and they informed me that the only time they took their guns out was to go to the firearms range for their quarterly competency test.

After six months in the unit we began to earn a reputation as being proactive, especially when we received a lot of press coverage after successfully closing down several major telemarketing operations. In spite of our successes, it was very difficult working in such close quarters with these detectives; tempers would flare when citizens became too demanding and the caseloads increased without additional manpower. My senior, Detective Glen, would often speak rudely to citizens on the telephone. When I brought it to his attention, he was not impressed and continued his behavior. When he hung up on a citizen after one of his tirades, I ordered him to meet me in the interview room. I pulled out a disciplinary report and the "written warning" I had previously given him and asked him what it was going to take for him to change his behavior. He said, "Why don't you tell me—you're the sergeant!"

I felt my blood pressure rise and I counted to ten, and then in a quiet voice I replied, "Let me think about that, and I will get back to you." I met with him at the end of the day and said, "I have made my decision." I handed him the disciplinary report reflecting a ten-hour suspension.

Glenn just smiled and said, "Is that all?" He signed the form and then extended his hand, saying, "You're the first supervisor who has ever had the guts to confront me, and I was out of line." He thanked me, and I never had another problem with him after that incident.

I learned a great deal about leadership working with tenured officers, and I was able to earn their respect by treating them fairly and being involved in their concerns. After a year in this assignment, a personnel notice came across my desk announcing a new police sergeant position heading up the first bike patrol. The notice said that the best candidates would possess good physical conditioning; excellent supervisory, leadership, and motivational skills; and an ability to direct proactive police patrol in an efficient, professional manner in high public visibility locations. I knew that I met these qualifications and was excited about pioneering a new method of policing in our city.

I did extensive research for my oral board and discovered that Seattle was the first police department to use police officers on bicycle patrol. They were extremely effective at reducing street crimes and dealing with vagrancy and other nuisance problems in the downtown district. I contacted Officer Grady, who was known as the guru of Seattle's bike patrol, and got his input on starting a unit in Las Vegas. I went to my oral board with a proposal to implement the unit, including suggestions for training and the officer selection process. My preparation and presentation during my interview impressed the board, and I was selected to be the sergeant of the first bike patrol. My male competitors were not happy that I had beaten them out of the position, and I began to hear sarcastic comments from them and others. The detectives I worked with thought I was crazy to leave my comfortable job in the office to go out on a bicycle and patrol the streets. I thought they were probably right, but I knew I was up to the challenge and looked forward to the new adventure.

I spent the first month with my new lieutenant purchasing bicycles and equipment for the new unit. I asked him what we were going to wear as a uniform. He looked at me with surprise and said, "We're going to cut off the uniform pants into shorts and wear our uniforms."

I paused and then said, "Sir, it's a hundred and twenty degrees in the summer months and down to thirty degrees in the winter. I think we are going to need to look at a more functional uniform."

"I'll let you take care of that," he said, "since that's a woman's department." I laughed and was eager to put together a uniform for the unit. Because I was an avid mountain bike rider, it was not difficult for me to assemble a professional and functional uniform that would meet our needs. I chose black padded bike riding shorts with utility pockets and spandex liners. We wore fluorescent yellow polo shirts with a cloth badge sown onto the breast pocket. The winter gear consisted of long spandex bike riding pants with a black and yellow lightweight ski jacket and wind pants with a black turtleneck sweater.

To model the new gear, I selected Rick, who had been a professional gymnast in college, and Chris, who had been a professional baseball player before joining the police department. When we walked into the sheriff's office, he sat back in his chair chomping on his cigar as I explained the function of the uniform and the mission of our new bike patrol unit. He asked the two officers to turn so he could see the back of the uniform. He stopped and said, "I'll take a pair of those legs." We all laughed, and I knew the uniforms were a hit with the sheriff. Everyone seemed impressed by our professional appearance.

Prior to kicking off the new bike patrol in May 1990, we invited Officer Grady to conduct a two-week training session for our officers. This guy was a competitive bicycle racer and was an animal on the fifty-mile training rides. At the end of our training session we had logged hundreds of miles and had become proficient at riding down stairs, doing "power slides," and a variety of tactical maneuvers with the bike. We were now ready to hit the streets on the Las Vegas strip, which had been plagued by gridlock traffic and gang shootings. I headed a squad of twelve officers organized into two-man teams. We divided the area into four sections, with one roving team and a transport team that drove the paddy wagon so we could transport prisoners to jail and haul additional equipment for the bikes.

One night, my partner, Rick, and I were patrolling in front of one of the major hotels on the Strip when we heard a woman scream, "He just stole my purse!" She was a tourist who had been walking on the sidewalk when a guy snuck up behind her and ripped her purse from her shoulder. We spotted him running down an alley next to the hotel, and the chase was on. We quickly closed in on the suspect, and riding up beside him, we yelled, "Stop! Police! You're under arrest!" The guy just kept running, and Rick signaled me to go ahead. I sprinted in front of the suspect and did a power slide, catching his feet and sending him tumbling over my bike. Rick grabbed him and put the handcuffs on, and we called for our paddy wagon to transport him to jail. Our bike patrol became well known in the jail because our prisoners always had black tire tread marks on their legs from our power slides.

We received a lot of notoriety being the first bike team in Las Vegas, and the television program COPS wanted to air an episode of our team. The officers were ecstatic at the thought of being movie stars. The show was approved to film my team over a two-week period and would follow us on patrol in a pickup truck carrying their camera equipment. One night Rick and I came across an ex-felon from Florida who was carrying an illegal knife in his back pocket. The man was uncooperative and refused to sit down even after I asked him several times, so I grabbed his arm to sit him down. As I pulled away he tried to elbow me in the face. I grabbed him by the throat and choked him out, as it turns out, on national television. It was a hit with the viewers, and we became celebrities. Tourists often recognized us and would yell, "Hey, you're the cops that were on that television show! Can we have your autograph?"

Being a bike cop was a lot of fun but demanding, so we had to stay in top form. I scheduled long training rides once a week to maintain fitness and readiness in performing our duties. One weekend we were invited to ride a hundred-mile fundraising race for charity. Our squad rode in formation the entire ride, completing the course in five hours.

Our unit became a model for others like it around the country. One way I shared our experience was to develop a bike patrol manual outlining our training and patrol procedures on the bicycles. Those manuals were then distributed to other police agencies all over the country. The uniform also became a model for other agencies, and my team and I received a commendation from my supervisor. It said, "Your commitment, enthusiasm, and imagination have contributed greatly to the success and recognition that this unit is now experiencing. I would be remiss if I didn't mention that the 'woman's touch' is certainly reflected in the fine fashion which is typified in the uniform selected for the Bike Patrol. The professionalism, effectiveness, morale, and commitment to excellence this unit exhibits are a true reflection of your supervisory efforts and ability. As your lieutenant, I'm proud to write this letter." At the end of our first year, all the officers received commendations for their performance in the unit and our success in lowering the crime rate.

While we continued to experience success in the unit, we had to work through animosity and jealousy from other patrol squads who thought we were getting too much recognition. I walked up to our office one afternoon and found a sign on the door that read: DYKE PATROL. It wasn't long after that I was approached by two officers from another station who told me they were offended by a comment made about me in the briefing room by another sergeant. They told me that my old buddy, Sergeant Dillon from the academy, had told a briefing room full of men about a crude and explicit sexual fantasy involving me.

It was evident that Dillon had not learned his lesson and was still as vulgar and offensive as he was in the academy. I later confronted Dillon, asking him if he had made that lewd comment about me in briefing. He told me he didn't know what I was talking about. I warned him that if he did not stop, I would file a formal complaint against him. He laughed and sped off in his patrol car.

The comments continued, and as had happened earlier in my police career, I began to experience problems with someone covering my radio transmissions by keying the microphone while I was talking. Since this created an extreme safety hazard, I knew it was time to file a complaint. I went to my chain of command and filed a sexual harassment complaint against Dillon. It was investigated, and he was found guilty on the charge. He was given an oral counseling and promoted to lieutenant a month later.

After two years in the unit, I decided it was time to move on. One day I received a telephone call from the inspections commander, whose unit was responsible for conducting line and staff inspections of all areas in the department. The commander informed me I had been recommended for this unit and the sheriff had endorsed my transfer. As part of this unit I would be working directly for the sheriff doing inspections. I was selected with three other sergeants and would now focus on the administrative side of policing, which would prepare me for the lieutenant's position when I became eligible.

I worked with Al and Ron, two great guys, and we all got along very well together. We would alternate lead positions because that was the most challenging position when confronting ranking officers with their unit's deficiencies. We inspected four areas: personnel, equipment, operations, and budget. We relied on the documentation provided and our personal observation while conducting the inspection. At the preinspection briefing, Al always put a transparency up on the wall that had a

Debra Gauthier

picture of the world and, beneath it, this message: *We don't want to change your world. We just want to change your oil.* Al had a dry sense of humor, and he always got a few nervous laughs when he did his presentation.

The exposure to the different challenges in all areas of the department was invaluable to me when I was testing for command staff. I essentially learned what not to do by the deficiencies we identified during the inspection process. One day I received a telephone call from the assistant sheriff who commanded the Investigative Division. He remembered me from the inspection of the Use of Force Board that he had implemented and said, "Sergeant, you really hit me hard on that inspection of my board. I like your tenacity, and I am looking for someone of your caliber to develop a new unit in my division." He explained that the homicide detectives did not have the time to properly investigate missing person cases, so he wanted to develop a new unit. I was honored that he had that much confidence in me to start this new unit, so I accepted his offer.

The next three months were spent working in Homicide, reviewing current and past missing person cases and compiling data in order to implement the new unit. I was given a small budget and allocated two detectives and an administrative assistant. I chose Larry and John, who had worked with me in another unit; I knew them to be like bulldogs when it came to investigating a case.

We formed an alliance with a nonprofit organization called "Child Seekers," that provided volunteers whenever there was a search for missing children. Our teamwork paid off when a young girl was abducted from her apartment complex; within minutes we had faxed the picture of the girl to Child Seekers, who quickly printed flyers and distributed them to the media. I set up checkpoints at intersections where the child was abducted.

With all the press and activity, the little girl was later released unharmed.

During this time I had taken the promotional examination for lieutenant for the second time and was disappointed to find the oral board members had rated me number eleven on the list. I didn't understand why I had received such a low score, and their comments did not justify the ranking. They were more concerned with how I looked rather than how I performed, with one rater writing, "She looks too young!" When I took the test I knew I was in trouble when one of the board members looked me up and down in a very demeaning manner. It was apparent that I had reached the "glass ceiling," and I felt more sure than ever that it might be a good time to re-explore the idea of going to law school.

I took the LSAT law school entrance examination and successfully passed. I then applied to five law schools and was accepted to the University of San Diego Law School, which was my brother-in-law's alma mater. I began to make plans to attend the fall semester and was surprised when I moved up to the number one position on the lieutenant's list because of some unexpected retirements. I did not allow this to get my hopes up and had decided not to take the lieutenant's test again.

Prior to going on vacation, I met with my lieutenant, who had been on the police department for thirty-six years and was considering retirement. At one point during the conversation I said to him, "Sir, why don't you retire so I can make lieutenant?" He just laughed, and I left his office. I went on vacation the next day to go snow skiing with some friends. I told my detectives that I would be skiing in Mammoth and not to bother me.

A few days into my ski trip, I was warming up in the lodge when I heard a message come over the intercom. The voice said, "Paging Lieutenant Debra Gauthier. Please call the front desk."

I looked at my friends and asked them, "Was that for me?"

They looked at each other and shrugged, I don't know, when the voice repeated the message. This time we all heard it, and I looked at my friends, saying, "That's a real sick joke, guys."

They said, "We didn't do that; you better check it out." I responded to the front desk and received the message from Larry and John at my office. I called the guys and said, "Did you call me?" They were laughing and affirmed they had called me. I asked them how they had found me, and they replied, "We are detectives!"

Now I laughed and said, "Okay, why did you call me?" They asked me if I wanted the good news first or the bad news. I requested the bad news first. Larry said, "Our lieutenant is retiring at the end of the year."

"Okay, what's the good news?"

"You're taking his place! "Congratulations, Lieutenant." I shouted and started jumping with joy. I was absolutely elated! Although law school had become more and more appealing to me over the years, my heart was still in police work, and I could not wait to get back to work. My friends treated me to a victory dinner that evening in celebration of my new promotion.

When I arrived in my office, I found a yellow message sheet with a pair of lieutenant's bars attached, and a note reading: *You wanted them, you got them. Congratulations!* I was promoted in January 1994, the same time that the new sheriff took office. I knew I was in trouble when I got my first assignment to work for a Captain Mike who was one of the sheriff's good old boys. This captain had worked on the sheriff's campaign and belonged to his inner circle; I had helped a friend that was running against this sheriff, and I was now on his "hit list" because I did not support him.

I was transferred to the Southwest Area Command as the area lieutenant for days and swing shift. Before I arrived at the station, I heard that Captain Mike had attended a briefing and had told the troops they would be getting me as their new lieutenant, and he disrespectfully told them I was not his choice. Without the honor and respect of my captain, I was doomed for problems with my staff.

As expected, the captain was less than welcoming and was very curt and formal in his demeanor. He intentionally failed to notify me of important meetings with the other lieutenants, which left me out of the loop and put me at a great disadvantage. One week before he left for a six-week vacation, he assigned me as the field commander for a major labor/union strike at the MGM Hotel on the Las Vegas Strip. I was still a probationary lieutenant, but was given no direction or assistance from him in order to succeed in this task. I did not let that stop me from pushing forward and went to work planning and organizing this event. I solicited the help of two other lieutenants, and we strategized an approach that would lead to a peaceful assembly. I had worked the Culinary Union strike in 1984, which had escalated into riots lasting for weeks. We had to work in four-man patrol cars working twelve-hour shifts seven days a week, and I knew that we could not afford either that kind of expense or the negative publicity to our city. We decided to hold meetings with the hotel and union representatives in an effort to avoid a recurrence of 1984 and mediate a solution that was agreeable to all parties involved. After many meetings we finally came to a workable solution.

We worked closely with the district attorney's office to obtain legal advice, and the command staff was pleased with the planned peaceful rally at the MGM Hotel. The union was permitted to walk onto the MGM property where hotel representatives advised them that they were trespassing. We then conducted a mass arrest and loaded all of the violators onto jail buses and transported them to a staging area, where they were issued a citation and released. We effectively arrested hundreds of protestors and avoided any violence or disturbance of the peace. When my captain returned from vacation, he did not even acknowledge my success and was angry when I received letters from the MGM president and union bosses thanking me and our officers for our professionalism and integrity.

That was only the beginning of my year from hell. It would be marked by many put-downs and offenses, including the captain's intentionally leaving me out of meetings and abruptly changing my days off, causing me to work extra hours without compensation. He transferred me from dayshift to graveyard and then back again, which was a great hardship as I was continually trying to adjust to the hours. I was transferred eight times in one year, and the additional stress that I was under began to take a toll on my health.

In addition to my supervisory responsibilities, I was tasked with watch commander duties several times a week. I would seldom see my captain on this shift, so I had to communicate with him through memorandums. In one of these memorandums I had notified my captain that I had been called to an extradition in Chicago and would be gone for three days and that I had made arrangements for another lieutenant to cover my watch commander duties while I was gone. When I returned, I was summoned to the captain's office, where he presented me with an Investigation of Complaint, saying he was investigating my violation of policy for leaving my watch commander duties unfulfilled. I explained that I had made arrangements with the other lieutenant, but the captain was not interested in hearing about that. He proceeded with a full-blown investigation and wrote me up for neglect of duty. I appealed the case to the deputy chief, showing him the memorandum that I had received from the lieutenant stating he would cover my watch commander duties. Evidently he had forgotten about the responsibility and was not called. The deputy chief overturned the discipline, and

I was cleared of wrongdoing, which only caused resentment and intensified the mistreatment of me by my captain.

I came to the end of my rope one day when I had a run-in with the captain over the misappropriation of donated monies for a new unit we were starting. I was trying to explain to him that another squad was using the equipment we had purchased, and he began to scream, "Don't you tell me about misappropriated funds, Lieutenant! Nobody is misappropriating anything." He would not listen to logic; I stood there until dismissed. When I walked out into the briefing room I realized everyone had heard the captain yelling. I retreated into the locker room and broke down in tears, embarrassed and hurt by how the captain had spoken to me.

The captain continued to use me to put out fires and address problems with sergeants working in his command, which put a lot of pressure on me and created hostility with the men. When he transferred me to graveyard, I had to deal with a sergeant and his officers who were going to the bar after their shift and drinking all day. Several officers had been involved in a drunken brawl, and our dayshift units had had to respond to break it up. I put the sergeant on notice, and he immediately went to the captain. The captain responded by transferring the sergeant from graveyard to dayshift, completely undermining my authority.

The weight of the captain's oppression was taking its toll on me. I met with him to explain my concerns, but he was not interested in hearing about any of it. I then asked to go above him to the deputy chief for help, and he said, "Go ahead." When I met with the chief, he told me that my captain had already met with him and that he was backing him. Anger at the injustice was creeping into my soul. I asked for a transfer from the command, and the chief replied, "You're a probationary lieutenant, so your transfer is denied." I pleaded with him to reconsider his decision, but I knew it was futile.

Debra Gauthier

During this time, because of my high profile in the community as a lieutenant, I was selected for the Las Vegas Chamber of Commerce Women of Achievement Award in 1995 and also chosen to be a member of the prestigious Leadership Las Vegas program sponsored by the Chamber of Commerce. I had also graduated from the Dale Carnegie Leadership training program that year and became an instructor for them. Because I was a member of several boards, some colleagues selected me to be a member of the Nevada Judicial Assessment Commission, and I was privileged to work on that panel for two years. My success in the community angered the sheriff, and he began looking for ways to get rid of me. I didn't want to believe it, but I discovered my greatest challenge was never the criminals on the streets but the criminally-minded on the police force.

It was disheartening to discover that some of the sergeants who worked under my captain had no sense of ethics. I became aware that one of my sergeants, Bobby, would call the secretary and tell her to change his status on the lineup, showing him as working when he was not. He would do this on my days off so I had no idea this was happening—that is, until I caught him in a restaurant in civilian clothes having breakfast on one of his working days. I checked with the secretary, and she told me that Bobby had instructed her to change the lineup to show him working. I asked her how many times he had done this, and she said, "I'm not sure of the number, but this is not the first time." I pulled the records and discovered five incidents where the lineup had been changed.

When Bobby returned to work, I confronted him and conducted a formal investigation. During the interview he said he was only joking with the secretary. Bobby had previously been an Internal Affairs investigator, so he knew the severity of his actions. I recommended suspending him for the number of hours that he had stolen from the department but was overturned by my captain. He said the punishment was too harsh and that he would only approve a written reprimand. I had to choose my battles and this was not one of them, so I administered the written reprimand and let Bobby know he had gotten off lightly. Bobby later went to the assistant sheriff and had the whole case overturned without even notifying me. He did not stop there but contacted two other sergeants who had been disciplined under my command; they went to their union and filed formal charges against me, demanding my demotion.

I notified my captain that I had had enough and that this was his responsibility because he had not supported me in my decision and left me vulnerable to attack. The case remained open, hanging over my head for many months. I finally filed a Title VII complaint for disparate treatment against the captain, and he was eventually transferred to the Communications Bureau. The case was suddenly closed, and I was exonerated from the charges.

Just when I thought I was going to get some relief, the deputy chief abruptly transferred me to work for my captain's best friend at the Southeast Area Command. This was another one of the good old boys and one of the sheriff's supporters, and I knew I was in trouble again. The first day my new captain, Steve, called me into his office and asked me, "You still want to work here?"

I thought that was a strange question to ask, but I replied, "Yes, sir."

"Good," he said, "You are being relieved of command and will be my administrative lieutenant and watch commander out on patrol." This meant I was to be the only lieutenant in patrol without any officers assigned to me, which was detrimental to my career. I was a laughing stock to the other commanders as my credibility and reputation were tarnished.

In spite of the adversity, I kept a good attitude, and I was just happy to be out on patrol again as a field lieutenant. One day I was out with the officers when I spotted several suspicious men in a residential area loading items onto a truck. They fled when I drove up, and I discovered the items were guns that had been stolen during several residential burglaries. I apprehended one of the suspects and directed backup officers to the other fleeing suspects. We were able to apprehend all of the suspects and recover all of the weapons.

On another afternoon, patrol units came on the radio and informed the dispatcher that they were in pursuit of a stolen vehicle out of California. I responded and monitored a fifty-mile pursuit of this California fugitive. I radioed officers in Overton to stop traffic on the freeway and lay out the road spikes. It worked, and the driver of the stolen vehicle drove over the spikes, blowing out all four tires. He came to an unwanted stop at the side of the road and was quickly taken into custody without incident.

Just when I was having fun, my captain informed me I would be going to the jail working mandatory twelve-hour shifts as a report-screening lieutenant. I thought, *You have got to be kidding!* Traditionally that would have been assigned to the junior lieutenant at the station, but my captain overrode tradition, and I was stuck with that duty. He told me my new shift started the next day and my days off had changed as well. I reported to the jail the next day at six a.m. as ordered and left at the end of the shift at six p.m. I never saw the light of day during my jail assignment, and it felt like I was in jail.

One morning I was riding in the elevator when an inmate looked me in the eyes and said, "I might be in jail, but at least I'm free." What an unusual thing to say. His words stopped me. I kept thinking about it later in my little office in the booking area. I did not realize it then, but that moment I was beginning an inner journey that would eventually change my life.

After several months, I was finally released from the jail assignment, and my captain agreed to give me a command. So he graciously assigned me sergeants who had either been a disciplinary problem or had a record of poor performance. I could already see a replay of the circumstances I had just endured with my previous captain. That morning I walked into my captain's office and said, "Sir, I feel like a pilot who has spent many years obtaining all the ratings and certifications to fly, and I am excited that I finally have been given a plane. However, I am in a dilemma because I know that if I fly that broken-down plane and it crashes, it will be said that I was a poor pilot. And if I refuse to fly the plane, then it will be said that I missed an opportunity because of my choice."

The captain laughed. "Congratulations on your plane, Lieutenant. Good luck!"

I recognized this as an opportunity—another test of my strength and character. I walked out of his office determined to make the sergeants into a successful, cohesive unit. I knew I had my work cut out for me. First, I relied on my Dale Carnegie training to motivate and build relationships with these officers. I was able to develop a rapport and good working relationship with all except one. He was the senior sergeant, Al, who went out of his way to disrespect me and challenge my authority. When I held staff meetings, Al intentionally missed them and refused to adopt my management plan. I chose not to fight him; instead, I focused on his positive qualities and recognized him for his leadership skills. He was embarrassed during one briefing when I read aloud in front of everyone a commendation I had written for him. Al had captured a bank robber who fled the scene in a taxicab, and I publicly congratulated him for his keen observation skills and quick response. He later thanked me for the commendation and told me I was the first lieutenant who had taken the time to recognize his performance. I knew this was a step in the right direction, and I looked forward to turning the situation into a win-win.

Debra Gauthier

I had been working with Captain Steve for about a year, and one morning I saw him sitting in a dark office with his winter coat on. I said, "Captain, are you okay?"

He looked at me with fear in his eyes and replied, "I'm just not feeling well." Steve asked me if I would mind taking over the command for him while he went home. It was the first time I had ever seen him take time off work. Soon I received a telephone call from the Internal Affairs commander summoning me to their office. There I met with Commander John, who told me that he was investigating a serious act of misconduct involving Captain Steve and another sergeant, Ron. He went on to tell me that I was a witness because my captain had given Ron, a friend of his, credit for the MGM Culinary Union tactical operation plan that I had developed. Evidently my captain had falsified Ron's performance appraisal to help him get promoted to lieutenant. Commander John requested all of my documentation and ordered me to give a statement. I said, "John, we're friends and I would love to help you, but I am not going to testify against my captain." I explained everything I had gone through with my previous captain, but John was not interested in hearing it.

"I'll make it formal and give you a written notification for tomorrow's interview," John said. When I drove back to the station, there was a part of me that wanted to see my captain punished for all of the hurt he had caused me by treating me so unfairly, but there was another part that did not care to be used to take out another officer.

I cooperated with Internal Affairs, giving them a statement and the evidence they requested. My captain told me he had a meeting with Sheriff Keller, who was a good friend of his, and was told he was only going to get some hours for discipline. Commander John held a grudge against Ron, the sergeant my captain had helped, and he was determined to take him down. I remember John telling me that first day that he would go through my captain to get Ron the sergeant for causing him problems when he was working in Narcotics. Commander John completed his investigation, and the sergeant was removed from his second-place position on the lieutenant's promotional list as discipline. Keller went against his word and demoted my captain back to a lieutenant; Steve was crushed by the betrayal of the sheriff and would harbor bitter resentment for many years.

I saw a side of John I had never seen before. I remembered working with him as a rookie officer, and he had always showed compassion and respect to others. John wasn't satisfied merely with the sergeant's loss of position on the promotional list, so he attempted to hurt him further by orchestrating another investigation—this one alleging that this sergeant had used the department's equipment and time to study for the test.

This new investigation resulted in the sergeant's demotion to police officer. He was assigned to the desk and eventually fired for a subsequent violation of policy. When I testified at the civil service hearing of Captain Steve and Sergeant Ron, the evidence that was presented was very damaging to their case. Even though I had no great love for either of them, I felt terrible when I walked past their families, who were sitting in the audience. I recognized my captain's two brothers who were also police officers and saw the hurt in their eyes as they watched their brother's career go down the tubes. Then I walked into the hallway, where Commander John smiled and said, "Good job in there!" I thought how coldhearted and vengeful this man had become, and my heart was sickened.

I carried the burden of being maliciously used against brother officers and was deposed for their civil action against the department. When their attorney asked me if I feared retaliation as a result of my testimony, I replied, "Sir, over the last few years I have had my telephone illegally monitored, intruders in my home, my life threatened, so to answer your question, yes!" I felt like I was swimming in a tank with sharks and they were just waiting for any scent of blood so they could go into another frenzied attack. There was no loyalty among these men, and they had no conscience about taking out their own to get at their target.

Shattered Family, Broken Life

If your first concern is to look after yourself, you'll
never find yourself. But if you forget about yourself
and look to me, you'll find both yourself and me.

Matthew 10:39

My mother and father met in Rhode Island when my dad was
in the air force. They were married age nineteen, and a year after
they were married my dad received orders to Holloman Air
Force Base in Alamogordo, New Mexico. I was born there in
1957, and a year later my dad was transferred to Craig Air Force
Base in Selma, Alabama. While in Alabama my mom went to
work, and her mother, an immigrant from Poland, took care of
me. She spoke in her native Polish language, which became my
first language.

When I was two years old and my mother was pregnant with
my sister Doreen, my dad decided to take us on a picnic to a
nearby park surrounded by a lake. I was playing near the dock
when my mother became worried and told my dad to go and get
me. My dad brushed her off, saying I would be all right. Sure
enough, a few minutes later I ran full speed across the deck and
right off the edge into the water. My mother screamed in horror
as my dad frantically ran to rescue me.

My sister Doreen was born in 1959, and a year later my dad
received orders to Stead Air Force Base in Reno, Nevada. I
remember driving across country with my little sister, uncertain
of what lay ahead but feeling safe because my dad was there.

My brother Joseph was born in Reno in 1962, and soon my dad received orders to Laos, Thailand, and then to Vietnam to fight in the war. He did two tours and was gone for over a year. In between tours he would be gone on temporary duty assignments for months at a time. I began to notice when my dad was home he would shut off from the family and he began to drink heavily, which caused him to break out in violent rages. With my dad gone all the time I began to feel a deep sense of abandonment.

In 1963 my dad received orders to Nellis Air Force Base in Las Vegas, Nevada. The time away and his drinking began to take a toll on my parents' relationship, so my mother decided to stay in Reno with her children. Mom worked at a hotel in downtown Reno as the head cashier and made good money. My father and mother continued to fight about the decision to move, and just before it was time to leave, my mother got ill with pneumonia and had to be hospitalized.

While my mother was in the hospital, the neighbor called her and told her my dad had a moving van in front of the house and was moving all of our belongings. This forced my mother to leave the hospital, which released her, but she was still very sick. My mother had to lie in the back seat of the van while my dad drove us across the state. These were turbulent years as my dad continued to drink heavily and violently abuse my mother.

My brother Steve was born six years after we arrived in Las Vegas. There was a fifth sibling, but that young life was eliminated through an abortion. I remember my mom's anger when she discovered that she was pregnant again. Abortions were illegal back then, so she had to go to some back alley clinic where the procedure was performed in secret. She came home that night pale and in agonizing pain. I later heard her crying in her bedroom, so I imagined that it had not been easy for her. She never talked about it, and it was as if it had never happened.

Debra Gauthier

The fighting between my dad and mom continued to escalate and my mother's suspicions grew as my dad spent hours after work at the bar. One night my mother decided to follow him to the bar, so she loaded her small children into the car and parked down the street. It was late, and we sleepily sat in the back when my mother spotted my dad walking out of the bar holding hands with another woman. A jealous rage rose up in my mother and I saw a part of her that shocked me. She bolted from the car, running up to them and grabbing the woman by the hair as she beat her in the face with her fist, yelling profanities. I watched in horror as my little brothers and sister began to cry.

My dad continued drinking, and it became so bad that my dog would hear his car coming down the street and hide under my bed. It was the same pattern every night with my dad coming in late, followed by his yelling because his dinner was cold. My mother would lash back at him in anger, and then the dishes would start flying, crashing against the wall, with my dad beating my mom. The next morning my mother would quietly walk into the kitchen wearing sunglasses to cover her black eyes, and I could see her tear-stained, bruised cheeks and swollen lip. Living in this violent environment created many fears and insecurities in me and my siblings.

One particular event deeply wounded my ten-year-old soul and opened the door to evil in my life. My dad had come in late, like many other nights, and I was already in bed. I could hear arguing in the kitchen, and then it got mysteriously quiet. I got up out of bed and walked down the hall toward the kitchen. The light was on, but there was a deafening silence. As I peered around the corner I saw my six-foot-two father crouched over my five-foot-two mother, choking the life out of her. Her face and fingernails were blue, and her eyes were bulging. I was horrified, and in a panic I ran to the stove, grabbing the iron skillet, and with all my strength I hit my dad on the back of his head.

It stunned him, and he got up off my mother and turned his drunken rage toward me.

The next thing I remember is lying on the floor and looking up at my mother, who was still crying and wondering what had happened. My father hit me so hard I crashed into the wall and was knocked unconscious. He finally left the house, and my mother realized that if she did not get us out of there, he would certainly kill her. This was enough for my mother to take action, and she went to the base commander and had my dad kicked off the base. We lived on base another six months while my mom began the divorce proceedings. My dad went AWOL and began living with another woman.

We moved off base into a two-bedroom apartment where my brother Steve was born. My mother struggled to support us and had to work two jobs. One night my mother decided to go out with a girlfriend for a few hours. She told me to sleep in her bed and not answer the door for anyone. I was awakened by a pounding on the front door, and my heart was struck with terror when I heard my dad's drunken voice calling out to my mother and ordering her to open the door.

I hid my siblings under the covers and hoped he would leave. After what seemed like a long time, the pounding and yelling stopped. We thought he had left until the glass from the bedroom window came crashing in on us. I jumped out of bed and frantically gathered up my infant brother, Steve, and my sister Doreen and brother Joe, and we quickly hid in the closet.

A few minutes later there was a knock on the front door, and I heard the sound of keys turning in the lock. We were trembling in fear as I muffled the cries of my infant brother. We heard someone walking around the apartment and finally come into the bedroom. We cringed as the closet door opened, and a stern-looking police officer stood towering over us. In a gruff voice he told us to get out of the closet and instructed me to get my

Debra Gauthier

siblings dressed. I was shaking so badly it was hard to get dressed as my sister and brothers cried hysterically. I told the officer we could not leave, and he ignored me and led us out to his patrol car. As I sat in the back on the cold vinyl seats, holding my infant brother with my sister and brother pressed against me, I fought back the tears, wanting to be strong for them.

When we arrived at Child Haven, a county facility for abandoned and abused children, my two brothers were placed on one side of the facility, leaving my sister and me without them. We would not see them again until months later. My sister and I were led to a large room filled with bunk beds. I lay there in shock amid the sound of muffled cries from other little girls as I felt the sting of abandonment and the terror of the unknown.

We were in the facility for several months as my mother fought to regain custody of us. When we were finally released back to our mother, we moved to a neighborhood with other military families living there. My dad did not pay child support, which forced my mother to work two jobs to try to provide for us. My mother met a wonderful Christian couple, Jerry and Joanne, who offered to babysit while my mother continued to work. She would come home tired after working on her feet all day, and this couple would often have dinner ready and invite us to join them. There was such peace in their home, and everyone had joy, which was so foreign to us.

A few months later the company that my mother worked for moved, so she had to find another job. She applied for a job at the mall along with another woman by the name of Alice. They both got the job and became close friends. Alice and her husband were strong Christians, and they too offered to take care of my siblings and me as my mother worked. Looking back, it is amazing how God placed his people around us during very difficult times. Even with their support and prayers, the wounds I carried from the abusive, fearful environment I had lived in began to take a toll on me. I began to act out in rebellion and ran away from home several times. I started to hang out with the wrong crowd and before long was drinking and taking drugs to numb the pain of my childhood.

One night my best friend, Olga, and I decided to run away to California. We packed our things and headed to the highway to hitch a ride. It wasn't long before we were picked up by an older guy. It was a miracle that we were not raped or killed, but we ended up in California and lived with a couple who were trafficking drugs at a local high school. They would send us into the high school to sell drugs, and we lived on a constant high. Little did we know that the couple was under police surveillance, and early one morning the police raided their house and we ended up in a juvenile detention center.

We were transported back to Las Vegas, and my mother was ready to sign the papers to have me sent to the youth facility until I was eighteen years old. At the time I was fifteen years old, and my mother had given up on me. I realized that unless I made a choice to change, I was facing a life behind bars. I begged my mother to give me one more chance, and to my surprise, she agreed. I went home and started back to school, committed to turn my grades around so I could go to college.

While attending high school I worked part time to help at home financially. At the age of sixteen I applied for a summer position as the secretary for the Department of Civil Defense in the City of North Las Vegas. I was interviewed by Captain Munsell, a retired US Marine who was like a godsend in my life. I told him I knew shorthand, which was required for the job, and after hiring me the captain realized I did not have that skill when I kept asking him to repeat himself during dictation. In his kindness the captain signed me up for a shorthand class and patiently dictated his letters very slowly so I could take notes in longhand.

Debra Gauthier

Captain Munsell taught me many valuable things about integrity and character through his actions. He was strict but very gracious. I admired his leadership and the wonderful way he could capture an audience during his speeches. He invested more in me those few months than anyone else ever did in my whole life. This man was a shining light in my life, and he filled a longing in my heart for my dad.

When the summer was over and my job ended, I headed back to finish my senior year of high school. I continued to visit Captain Munsell and his wife and developed a close relationship with them. They told me I was like the daughter they were unable to have. The captain lived on a ranch, and I looked forward to working in the fields with him or canning fruit with his wife in the kitchen.

Competing in sports was always a big part of my life and provided the foundation to excel in my law enforcement career. While on the police department, I competed in the annual Nevada Police Olympics and won gold medals in track and field and swimming events. I was also involved in the annual Challenge Cup, a running race that we coordinated with the Los Angeles Police Department. Our department had a team in which each member ran a leg of the relay race beginning in California, with the finish line at the Hacienda Hotel in Las Vegas a hundred and twenty miles away. I ran the leg coming into the valley from Pahrump, which was a fast downhill course approximately seven miles long. The race would begin in the afternoon, and the relay teams would run through the night. Each year our team became more competitive with the California teams, and in 1989 we ranked in fourth place, ahead of many others.

I also competed in our department's Brass Challenge, a race that was run in the Valley of Fire each year. The "brass," or high-ranking members of the police department, ran against the officers in relay teams. One year the department decided to include a bicycle relay race that included an off-road course through the canyons of the Valley of Fire. I was teamed up with an officer, Dan, who rode the first leg of the course, which began at the visitor's center. He was going to ride on the roadway, approximately forty miles to the little town of Overton where he would pass off the baton to me, and I would begin the twenty-five-mile off-road portion of the course.

The race was run in mid-September, and Dan and I began to train in August. We decided to ride the course early one morning and met at the visitor's center in the Valley of Fire at five a.m. As soon as the sun began to rise, we took off on the course together, riding our mountain bikes. We had enough water to sustain us during the race, and we were wearing bicycle-racing attire. I wore a bright yellow bandana, helmet, and a spandex one-piece race suit, and we carried no extra provisions. We were timing ourselves and wanted to get an idea of where we stood with the competition and what we would need to work on before the race.

Kenny, a friend with whom I had gone through the academy, was the resident police officer in Overton, Nevada. He had marked the off-road portion of the course using bright-colored ribbons, but he had failed to tell me he had laid out two courses—one of them very treacherous and dangerous. I telephoned Kenny the day before we were going to ride the course and arranged to have him pick us up at the finish line and take us back to our vehicles at the visitor's center.

Everything went very smoothly on the road portion of the course, and we arrived in Overton in record time. We left the roadway and began riding on a dirt road leading to the trail that would take us through the back part of the Valley of Fire. It was midmorning when we began our trek, and the heat of the day was intensifying. There was a point where the two courses crossed, and Dan and I got on the wrong one. We discovered this was not going to be the actual race course as we found ourselves trudging through deep sand in the canyons. As we began walking our bikes, we realized the end of every canyon only revealed another hill. Soon the terrain all began to look the same. It hit us then—we were lost. Dan had a flat tire, and we both were growing very weary at this point. It was approximately eleven a.m., and we ran out of water as we walked our bikes through the sand. Dan wasn't looking too good, and I was getting lightheaded, so I said, "Let's find a shady rock and sit out the heat of the day and wait for help." Dan agreed, and we walked for another mile until we found a place against a canyon wall that provided cover from the now blazing sun.

It wasn't long before I had difficulty swallowing due to dehydration. Dan was suffering from heat exhaustion, and I was feeling the effects of this as well. I began to wonder if we were going to make it through this ordeal when Dan said, "It looks like we're going to be spending the night."

He made this little smirk, and I replied, "If we do, you're going to sleep over there." I thought I would get back at Dan and put a little humor into the situation to break the tension. I said to Dan, "Do you know that the barrel cactus has water in it?"

"You're kidding," he said.

"It's true," I lied with a straight face. "I learned about it when I took a desert survival class in college." That part was true, but I knew there had been no rain in this area for months and the cactus would be dry.

Dan took the bait; He crawled over to a cactus and, taking his pocketknife in hand, cut it open. "This looks dry," he said.

"You have to suck on the inside to get the liquid out," I told him. He bought my line and put the piece of cactus up to his lips and began to suck on it when I heard him scream out in pain. I looked at him and saw the cactus needles sticking out of his lip. I laughed so hard my sides ached. He crawled back over to the shade and lay there in discouragement. I finally apologized for my practical joke.

The time dragged on, and we both began to get ill from the heat and the effects of severe dehydration and Dan's cactus wounds. Ken was waiting for us at the finish line and began to get concerned when we did not arrive at the scheduled time. He waited for over an hour and then radioed to our dispatcher that we were lost in the Valley of Fire and he would he conducting a search. Ken took his four-wheel-drive police vehicle and drove the course that we were supposed to have been on. When he did not find us, he began to get worried.

By this time it was late afternoon, and I knew the sun would be going down in a couple of hours. I told Dan I was going to try to hike out of the canyon and go for help as soon as the sun was lower in the sky. Dan was semiconscious at this time, and I was really worried about him. My tongue was swollen in my mouth, making it very difficult to swallow. I was beginning to realize that dying of thirst was a very slow and agonizing process. I fought off fear and ventured out as the sun began to set behind the mountains. I walked along a trail for several miles while it began to grow dark. As I walked, I heard the sound of rattle-snakes; it dawned on me that they come out at night to hunt. The hair was standing up on my neck. Suddenly, in the distance I heard the sound of a helicopter coming toward me. I quickly climbed to the top of a hill and began to wave my yellow ban-dana when I could see the spotlight of the helicopter scanning the desert in front of me.

The helicopter flew right over my head and did not even see me. My heart sank, and discouragement began to set in until I saw the helicopter circle back toward me. Evidently, the copi-lot had seen our bicycles, which were lying in an open area. I watched in excitement as the helicopter landed and the officers loaded Dan on board. They took off and flew by me again as they headed toward the visitor's center, where an ambulance was waiting. I stayed on top of the hill and waited for the return of the helicopter. I hoped that Dan was able to tell them that I was on foot and the direction that I had gone. Before long I heard the helicopter and saw the spotlight. This time they circled over the area where I stood and finally spotted me on the hilltop. They landed in an open area, and I climbed down the hill and was met by one of the rescue officers. He said, "It's good to see you, ma'am," and gave me a much-needed drink of water. I never knew how good water tasted until that moment. I was flown out of the canyon, and we landed at the visitor's center. Dan was rushed to the hospital, suffering from heat stroke, and I spent time resting before I guided the rangers to where our bikes were still lying in the desert. There was no way I was going to leave our expensive bikes in that desert.

When I got home at two a.m., I found several messages on my telephone recorder from the police dispatcher and other officers who were looking for me. I could hear the worry in their voices, and many expressed their deep concern for my well-being. It took a couple of days to recover from the effects of heat exhaustion. When I went back to work I found a missing person report on my desk with Dan and I listed as the victims. There were signs pointing to water bottles all over the office. I laughed so hard and was grateful we had survived. A month later our training and survival test paid off as Dan and I finished the race in second place. And best of all, we lived to tell about it.

Academy Inspection as Rookie

Academy Graduation with Sheriff & Captain

Bike Patrol Squad

Bike Patrol Sergeant

Lieutenant Promotion

20 Years of Service

Patrol Sergeant

Field Training Squad

Field Training Squad

Academy Inspection

Sergeant and Officers

Patrol Squad

Light in the Midst of the Storm

Suddenly, God, your light floods my path, God drives out the darkness.

2 Samuel 22:29

Living in the desert all my life, I was accustomed to storms being a rare occurrence, and when they came, they hit hard. One afternoon I was on patrol when a fierce storm entered the valley, and within minutes, the streets flowed like rivers. I was dispatched to a vehicle trapped in the flood waters behind the strip. When I arrived, I saw a woman with her two small children terrorized as they sat in the stalled car with the waters rising quickly around them. I retrieved a cable from my trunk and yelled to a couple of guys to hold on to me as I waded out to the car. My boots filled with water, and my thick wool pants helped anchor me to the ground as I quickly made my way to the stranded vehicle. I grabbed the two little girls out of the window, and the mother followed, all three of them tightly holding on to me as the two men pulled us to the curb.

Within minutes of reaching safety we watched in horror as their car began to shake under the force of the waters and tumble over the edge of the street, which now had given way and gushed like a waterfall. The car succumbed under the water's powerful force, and we knew that this mother and her two children would have surely drowned.

That's exactly how it felt when the first fierce storm of my life hit me unexpectedly and threatened to carry me away. During my teen years I excelled in sports and joined a diving team at the local YMCA. Gary, my coach and a collegiate champion diver from Arizona State University, was firm but gentle. I grew close to him and his wife, Cindy, as we spent time together traveling to diving meets, and they became very precious to me. I watched as this dear man, a father of five children, coped with his wife's terminal cancer. I was amazed at his focus; he never let what he was going through affect his coaching. He was always there for us despite the pain in his own life. I had not seen that modeled in my life, so this was all new and amazing to me.

Gary and Cindy had helped me prepare for college and receive an athletic scholarship in diving to his alma mater. Cindy even made arrangements for me to join the same sorority of which she was a member while attending college. The spring before I was to leave for college, Gary's wife lost her battle with cancer and died. I wept at her funeral and felt a deep sense of grief for my coach and his children. I wondered why God would take such a wonderful woman before her time, leaving five children without a mother.

That summer I would face my own battle when my coach spotted a suspicious mole on the middle of my back. He told me to have it checked before we left that weekend for a diving competition. A few days later I got a call from the doctor; he told me he wanted to see me and my mother in his office as soon as possible. We drove in silence to the medical building as fears raced through my mind. My dreams of college and career flashed before my eyes. I thought, *How can this be happening when things are just beginning to turn around in my life?* Upon arrival, we sat in nervous anticipation as the doctor came in, sat down at his desk while grabbing a file, and with a look of concern on his face, gently broke the news to us. He said I had been diagnosed with malignant melanoma and it was in the advanced stages. He told us the survival rate was about 20–40 percent. I looked at him in disbelief as my mother began to cry. "How can that be?" I yelled out. "I'm in the best shape of my life!" He told us that melanoma was considered the "black widow" of the cancers because once you showed symptoms of being sick, it was usually too late.

I was immediately placed in the hospital for a series of tests and prepared for surgery and chemotherapy. I was still in a state of shock and fighting back the fear of possibly facing death. One evening I was sitting in the window sill of the hospital room, looking out over the traffic down below, and I began to cry. My life was just starting to turn around and I didn't understand why it had to end like this. I was angry at the injustice of the situation and at God for allowing it to happen. With my mind racing, I could not take it any longer, so I quickly got dressed and snuck out of the hospital. I took off running through the streets of the neighborhood and, finally, out into the desert as the sun was setting behind the mountains. I ran as fast and hard as I could until I had nothing left. I fell to my knees and began to cry as I begged God to spare my life. I told Him I would do anything for Him if He would let me live. I had been raised Catholic, so I knew there was a God; I just didn't know him. At that very instant that I asked God to save me, I felt an incredible flood of peace and love come over me. I knew at that moment that I would certainly not die but live.

During surgery the doctor cut out a section of my back the size of a basketball. This left me with a scar over twelve inches long. As I recovered from the surgery, a friend came by the hospital and brought me books about cancer and alternative healing techniques. I had been considering traditional and nontraditional medical treatments and made the decision to visit a clinic in Mexico to go through a detoxification program instead of poisoning my body with the drugs of chemotherapy. The oncologist told me I was foolish to turn down their treatment and would probably not survive. But I remembered my plea to God to spare my life, and I felt the same peace about pursuing this alternative cancer treatment. I had always been warned that if you messed up, God would get you. But I began to believe that God could actually be kind and caring.

The first of many storms I would endure during my twenty-one-year law-enforcement career occurred when I was teaching a report-writing class in the Police Academy. At the time I was mentoring Karen, a female officer who had approached me one day, telling me several women recruits were being harassed by the academy staff and were planning to quit. She asked if I would mind giving the staff a pep talk during break. I remembered what I had gone through as a new recruit, so I was more than happy to encourage the women. We met in the locker room, and I shared my story, encouraging them not to quit. Karen was present during the meeting and offered encouragement as well.

A few days later, the training commander, Richard, telephoned me to say that I was under investigation for "Subversive Acts against the Department and Disharmony." I was shocked and asked him what the basis for the allegations was. He accused me of holding a "secret meeting" in the women's locker room and of "creating dissension between the men and women in the class." I told him I did meet with the women recruits and had offered some encouragement and my intent was not to cause any disharmony but rather to repair rifts that had occurred. Again, he was not interested in my side of the story and promptly removed me from all teaching positions, including the Field Training Program. I was angry and said, "You have no right to destroy my credibility as an instructor and disrupt my squad and position based on rumor and speculation."

Before the matter was adjudicated I was transferred from my training squad back to the Northwest Area Command, working the graveyard shift. The irony of the whole situation is that the man who replaced me as sergeant and the lieutenant led the investigation and used Karen against me as a witness. The women in the academy class, who were already stressed and considering resigning, were now entwined in this web of deception and lies. I felt betrayed by both the academy staff and Karen. The situation created animosity between us, and she harbored a vendetta against me for years. The situation sort of fizzled, and after several months I was informed I had received an oral reprimand for creating "disharmony," and the matter was closed. The matter with Karen I would later discover was not closed.

After my demotion in 1997 I went back to work, to the surprise of my captain and chief, who expected me to quit. The harassment continued when the captain told me I would not have a squad assigned to me and I was to work as a police officer. When I walked into the patrol briefing room, I was met with silence and cold stares from the officers, who had been told I was quitting. I wore a sergeant's uniform again after being a lieutenant for five years, and was now the only sergeant without a squad and no equipment to do my job.

I retreated to the locker room and broke down in tears, overwhelmed by the loss and pain of humiliation. It seemed that no matter how hard I tried, no matter how I held to my principles, I could not succeed. I felt crushed at every turn, as if everything in the universe was conspiring to bring me down. The discouragement I felt was as thick as a wet, heavy fog. I drove around on patrol in shock most of the time, barely able to function even in the simplest tasks. I appealed my decision to Dick, the undersheriff, who twisted the words of my attorney, saying that he agreed I had retaliated against Chuck. My attorney had made an analogy for the sake of argument, saying, "Even if she had retaliated against Chuck, you have chosen the harshest form of discipline short of termination, which violates the whole concept of progressive discipline." I was shocked by the cold, harsh behavior of the undersheriff towards my attorney and me. He said, "She will never harm anyone else again."

The things he was saying did not even make sense, and I finally broke under the pressure, abruptly leaving the office. The undersheriff told my attorney, "I ought to fire her for insubordination!" Even my attorney, who has practiced labor law for years, had never seen anything like this. We elected to take our appeal to the next level.

I was faced with another difficult challenge during the month of September when I had to make a decision whether to appear at the Las Vegas Chamber of Commerce Community Achievement Awards. Members of my community had nominated me as a finalist for Outstanding Public Service. I had decided not to go, but my doctor and family encouraged me, saying I would regret not going. I will never forget that night sitting in the large ballroom with my family and friends when the spotlight came on me. The announcer said, "Welcome this year's recipient for outstanding public service, Debra Gauthier." The applause sounded like thunder, and I walked to the stage like I was in the clouds. I received the award and looked out at the audience; all I could see was the bright light. I again felt the overwhelming wave of love and peace that had come over me in my bedroom that night I had prayed. I gave a short speech, thanking my community for their confidence and appreciation of my service, and then dedicated the award to my mother, who had encouraged me to become a police officer.

The spotlight moved to my mother, who wept as my brother Steve comforted her. This ordeal I was going through had been just as hard on my family as it was on me. I spotted the sheriff and undersheriff seated in the audience, and I was sickened by their smirks as I walked back to my chair. To be betrayed by my own brothers was the deepest kind of hurt anyone I could possibly suffer; it cut to the bone. It reminded me of a story I had read in the Bible about Joseph. His father favored him over his brothers, which caused jealousy and resentment between the siblings and him. When Joseph shared a dream with his brothers, they conspired to kill him. They ended up throwing him in a pit and selling him into slavery. I felt a lot like Joseph—I had shared my dream of becoming a captain with my brothers, who then conspired against me and killed my career.

In December, the civil service hearing of my appeal began. I would now be going before a board that was controlled by the sheriff. We prepared our position, and I testified for seven hours before this board, explaining everything I had done while in my position as the bureau commander. My attorney presented evidence of commendations I was given for my leadership abilities and evaluations that reflected my competence and character over my twenty years in service. The only discipline in my file was an oral reprimand for a traffic accident. My attorney presented a copy of my evaluation from the first deputy chief I had worked for as a bureau commander. He had rated me commendable in all areas of leadership. The most telling evidence was the comments received from the assessors in the captain's assessment center. Comments included "excellent communication skills," "outstanding professional and educational development," and a "participative manager who leads by example, used persuasion rather than hard line approach." The assessors noted my greatest strengths in the areas of conflict resolution ability, decision making, personnel/resource management, preparation for job, and sensitivity. The assessors, who were commanders and majors from other agencies, told the sheriff they would love to have me on their own police departments as a captain.

One afternoon, in the midst of this fierce storm I was out riding my mountain bike in the Red Rock Canyons and was coming very fast down a narrow canyon. Two guys were coming up the canyon, and I had no way to avoid hitting them. I had to act in a split second. I grabbed my front disc brakes and careened over the handle bars. Because I was still clipped into my pedals, I took the full impact on my left shoulder when I slammed into the hard ground. I groaned in pain as I struggled to get loose from my bike when a couple I was riding with came to help. Bobby said, "Look at your shoulder; I think it's broken." I looked down and saw my clavicle, which had been snapped off at the bone and was almost protruding out of the skin. My left arm dangled as we tied a bandana around my neck to sling my arm. My right hand was also broken in the fall, so I was left with no functioning arms. I walked several miles in shock out of the canyon while Bobby pushed my bike and his wife helped me.

I was rushed to the hospital, where doctors wrapped my arm around my body, shot me full of painkillers, and sent me home to await surgery a few days later. My clavicle was pinned back onto my shoulder, leaving two steel pins sticking outside of my skin. Though my arm was in a sling, every motion caused excruciating pain in my shoulder. Doctors put my right arm in a cast just below my elbow to aid healing of an avulsion fracture to my right thumb. Without use of my arms, I couldn't take care of even my basic needs. My mother stayed with me the first few days after surgery, and several friends stopped by throughout the week to help care for me. I wasn't able to feed myself because the cast prevented me from holding anything in my right hand. I had reached the end of myself and sat in the presence of God, listening.

I appeared at the civil service hearing with my left arm wrapped around my body and right hand in a cast; it was physically difficult sitting through hours of witness testimonies. My attorney presented our case in one day, calling six witnesses who were directly involved in the situation. The department, on the other hand, hired expensive private attorneys to defend their position, calling eighteen witnesses and allowing testimony of hearsay and gossip to support their retaliation claim. They went

Debra Gauthier

all the way back to my academy days in an attempt to portray me as the villain. The sergeant whom I had written the commendation for testified that I intimidated him to the point that he was unable to do his job. I sat through the ten- to twelve-hour hearings over the next three months while the department attorneys called their witnesses. The pain of listening to the lies of men I had helped was more painful than my physical injuries. It became apparent that the board was siding with the department. The undersheriff testified, saying, "I knew her when she was a rookie officer on the 'black glove' squad terrorizing citizens." He told lie after lie in a matter-of-fact way and was a master at deception.

It wasn't bad enough to go through this mockery of a trial and endure the pain of listening to the lies, but the story was aired on all of the local television stations and was front page news in the local paper. I watched a news clip of the closing arguments showing me in tears before the board, and I switched off the television and cried myself to sleep. To no one's surprise, the board ruled against me and upheld my demotion to sergeant. Elgin, an African American businessman and the chairman of the board, was the only one who disagreed with the decision to demote me. In his final argument he pointed out that I was a manager dealing with a difficult employee. He also stated, "If the lieutenant committed a violation of policy, then the deputy chief was the one who should have been held accountable, because he was the one entrusted with the power to resolve the situation."

As I exited the auditorium, I looked out into the audience and saw the men who had caused my downfall. Dillon sat there proudly wearing his new lieutenant's bars and a big smile on his face. I felt sick to my stomach; I could not believe these men had gotten away with their evil plot. It was an obvious injustice—obvious to me and a few others, at least. A newspaper reporter even wrote that Chuck the sergeant had lied under oath regarding the number of covert tape recordings and also the timing of when he had actually started taping me. In spite of the controversy, the decision was upheld. Chuck had taped me for several months in an effort to build a case of retaliation against me. He had the deputy chief's blessing and Karen to help him put it all together.

This whole case had been cultivated in darkness, beginning with the covert tape recordings and the secret investigation made behind closed doors by the sheriff's handpicked Diversity Board. As I began to piece together the parts of this twisted puzzle, my first sergeant Tom told me he was sorry for what had happened to me and he wanted me to know he had defended me in the board meeting and that it was "nothing more than a witch hunt." Tom was a member of the board that had found me guilty of retaliation, and he told me that Karen was already discussing the discipline before they had even heard all of the evidence. Tom told me he had gone to the undersheriff and resigned his position on the Diversity Board because he did not want to be a part of something that was designed to needlessly destroy a career. Tom said that the undersheriff was unmoved by his decision, and even he felt aggrieved by this man's cold, calloused, dark heart.

The next storm came three years after my demotion, and coincidentally it happened on a stormy afternoon when I was preparing to secure after a day out on patrol. I had readjusted and settled into my old position as a patrol sergeant. Although the other sergeants and lieutenants kept their distance, I had the respect and support of my officers. It was hard to befriend anyone at this point because I did not trust anyone. As I headed into the station, an unlicensed car driven by a black male sped by, and I heard the Holy Spirit tell me to stop the car. I argued that it was time to go in and it was going to rain, but I felt pressured to obey. So I caught up to the car and initiated a vehicle stop. I

Debra Gauthier

approached the driver, a feminine-looking black man who was obviously in the homosexual lifestyle and was very nervous.

It began to rain, so I placed him in my police car as I waited for the tow truck. And then a wonderful thing happened. While I finished writing the traffic tickets, music from a Christian radio station began playing softly in the background. The man, Jessie, began to cry and told me he was tired of being gay. I gently asked if he wanted prayer, and he nodded his head yes. As I was praying, several backup officers arrived and took custody of this man, who had outstanding warrants.

A few days later on June 8, 2000, I was served with a complaint against me from the Narcotics Bureau. It was signed by Dillon, the officer who had been caught sexually harassing me in the Police Academy. He was now the lieutenant of Narcotics and still harbored a bitter resentment toward me. As I read the complaint I immediately recognized the name of the man whom I had stopped and prayed for. According to the complaint, I was under investigation for "interfering with police operations" and "public statements about controversial issues." The basis of the complaint revolved around the traffic stop I had made on Jessie, a narcotics informant. I found out later that he had told the Narcotics officer that I had prayed with him and the officer had taken that information to the lieutenant. The informant was only interested in getting his car back and had not initiated the complaint but was used as a pawn in the game to destroy my career.

Once again I found myself adrift in the storm, and instead of God moving the storm, He spoke peace to me while I endured it. I read in Matthew 5:11 that, "You're blessed when your commitment to God provokes persecution. The persecution drives you even deeper into God's kingdom," and I wondered why I did not feel blessed. Since God's ways are higher than ours, I knew all I could do was put my trust in him. I read once that "fear paralyzes and faith frees," so I put my faith in God and I continued to walk not by sight, but by faith. I was ordered to report to Internal Affairs where two investigators did their very best to entrap me with their leading line of questioning. Many of the questions made no sense to me because these men were trying to twist the words of the man with whom I had prayed. They asked me over and over again whether I had prayed with the man, and I confirmed it. Then they asked me if I held his hand and bowed my head, and I replied, "I had my ticket book and pen in my hand, and I may or may not have bowed my head. I don't recall." They asked me if it was common for me to close my eyes when I prayed, and I responded, "Not necessarily, I'm praying for both of you right now!" Their eyes began to dart back and forth as they fidgeted in their chairs, and they quickly moved on to another question.

The investigators asked me if I had ever prayed with anyone else while on duty. I told them that I had, and they asked how many. "I don't know. I wasn't counting," I replied. I asked them if it was wrong to pray for someone in need, because I had learned in the academy that we would play many roles as a police officer and one of them was clergy. They looked down at their paper and then asked again, "Have you prayed for anyone else while on duty?"

I replied again, "Yes," and they asked me to tell them about that. I recalled for them the story of a Vietnam veteran who had called for help when several ex-felons had taken over his trailer while he was in the hospital. As I drove up, I noticed a man sitting in a wheelchair with his little dog sitting loyally next to him. I spoke to my men who were handling the call and was told the man in the wheelchair was the one who had called for help. While they were busy with the ex-felons and removal of guns from the trailer, I approached the man in the wheelchair, smiled, and said, "What's your name?"

"Ron, ma'am," he replied.

"Hi, Ron," I said, "What's your dog's name?"

"Sassy." I learned that Ron had served in Vietnam and had lost his legs when a grenade exploded near him, killing his partner. I could see the pain and hopelessness in his eyes.

I looked down at him and said, "You're dying."

"Yes, I am," he replied.

"Do you know," I asked, "where you go when you die?"

"I hope I go to heaven," Ron said.

I asked Ron, "Do you know how to get to heaven?"

"Well," he said, "if you're a good person, I suppose you will go to heaven." I told him that was not true, that the only way to heaven was through God's Son, Jesus. I asked Ron if he knew Jesus, and he replied, "No, not really." I told him that God loved him so much that he sent his one and only Son, Jesus, to be a sacrifice for our sins and die in our place so that we could go to heaven and live with God. I asked Ron if he believed that God has resurrected Jesus from the dead and that he was alive now.

Ron replied, "I believe."

"Would you like to receive His gift of salvation and accept Jesus as your Lord and Savior?" I asked Ron. He looked up at me with tears in his eyes and said yes, he would. I got down on one knee and led Ron in a prayer where he accepted Jesus as his Lord and asked forgiveness for his sins. When I looked at Ron, I could see the life in his eyes and a wonderful glow come upon his face.

"I'm full of goose bumps," he said.

I laughed and said, "That's God's Spirit. He now lives on the inside of you."

The next morning, for some unknown reason I went directly out on patrol instead of doing my paperwork as I normally would. The reason became obvious to me when I saw the callback at Ron's trailer. I arrived first and met his two veteran buddies there. "Sarge," one of them said, "we knocked at Ron's trailer to help him get up like we normally do, but he didn't answer the door. We can hear Sassy barking, but we can't hear Ron." I saw Ron's wheelchair leaning against the porch where he typically parked it before dragging himself into his trailer. I noticed two small holes in the door, and I knew what had happened.

When my men arrived I showed them the two bullet holes, which had been fired from inside the trailer. "Kick the door, guys!" I directed. After announcing "Police," we entered and found Ron lying on the floor along with his .45 caliber pistol, his friend Sassy sitting loyally by him. It was a sad sight. Ron had shot himself in the head. His brains and blood had splattered all over the living room, even on Sassy. I had one of my men clean Sassy as I called for the coroner.

Then I spoke with Ron's friends and told them what had happened. They began to cry. Apparently Ron had just been released from veterans' hospital where he was on a suicide watch. They told me that Ron said he no longer wanted to live the way he was and endure the constant pain he was in. I told them Ron was in heaven with Jesus and asked them if they wanted to see him again. They both said yes. I asked them if they knew how to get to heaven, and they replied no. I shared the news of the gospel with Ron's two buddies that day, just as I had with Ron the previous day.

As I left the park I realized that God knew Ron was going to take his own life, and in his great mercy he provided Ron the opportunity to receive salvation. Jesus says in Revelation 3:20, "Look at me. I stand at the door. I knock. If you hear me call and open the door, I'll come right in and sit down to supper with you." Ron had opened the door and invited Jesus in that day, which would be his last on the earth.

When I was finished telling the story of Ron to the two investigators, they looked at each other amid a long period of silence. Finally, one of the investigators asked, "Is that the only other time you have prayed with someone on duty?"

I told them no, there was another time when two police officers who worked for me had been going through very difficult times in their personal lives. I explained how I had prayed with both of them too.

At the end of the interview I said, "When I took the oath of office as a police officer, it was under God, and it is still under him, and prayer is a part of the life of every Christian." I have spiritual discernment, so I knew who was behind this attack upon me and that the battle was indeed spiritual in nature, so I pressed on. In September, five months after I had stopped Jessie, the man whom I prayed for on the traffic stop, I was ordered to take a polygraph examination. It was clear that these men who were being used as instruments of Satan were building a termination case against me. My union representative advised me that this was an unlawful order because an officer is only obligated to take a polygraph when the complainant takes one and passes. The complainant in this case was not the man I had prayed for, but rather the lieutenant who had sexually harassed me. He was now fulfilling his vendetta against me and scoring points with the sheriff's administration by ordering me to take the polygraph. I was instructed to send a memorandum to my chain of command and inform them that the polygraph order was unlawful and to ask them how they wanted me to proceed.

I got my answer when I was summoned to Internal Affairs, where I was relieved of duty and a new investigation was opened for "gross insubordination." I was ordered again to take the polygraph or face immediate employment termination. I knew if I took the polygraph, they would manipulate the test results in a way that substantiated their case. If I refused, I would be fired for insubordination. Either way, they had successfully laid a trap for me. I got up from my chair, reached across the desk to shake their hands, and said, "As you judge, so will you be judged."

On Monday, October 2, 2000, at 9 a.m., I reported for the polygraph examination. A veteran officer whom I respected explained the procedure and asked me how much sleep I had gotten. "Under the circumstances," I replied, "not much, sir." He insisted on delaying the test so I could get the proper rest, but I said, "Postponing the test will only make matters worse because I know the motive behind this whole situation is aimed at my termination, regardless of the outcome of your test." The test went forward as planned, and the results came back inconclusive; the machine was reading the stress in my body. The administering officer said, "I am not going to allow the sheriff to use this as evidence against you, because it would be unfair." I shook his hand and told him, "God bless you."

I was ordered back to work, which would be short lived. About a month later, Mike, the captain whom I had filed a discrimination complaint against, was promoted to patrol commander, and his first order of business was to take the case from Internal Affairs and close the case against me using the inconclusive polygraph test as evidence that I was lying. I knew I would not have an opportunity to say good-bye to my men, so I wrote the following letter to them:

> Dear Squad NE22,
>
> I just wanted to take a moment to tell each of you what an honor it was serving with you guys. Your selfless dedication and commitment to our mission touched me. There were no stars among us, just a group of winning players. I hope that I was able to impress on each of you the importance of walking in integrity and doing your jobs with compassion. Never fear reaching out to help others because you never know what kind of impact that will have on someone's life. The Law Enforcement Code of Ethics says our fundamental duty is to

serve mankind; to safeguard lives and property; to protect the innocent against deception, the weak against oppression or intimidation, and the peaceful against violence or disorder, and to respect the Constitutional rights of all men to liberty, equality, and justice.

I came across this quote that Olympians live by: "If everyone agrees with everything you are doing, you are taking the path of least resistance. The path of least resistance makes rivers and people crooked. Olympians do what they know to be right and in the best interest of long-term success, not what is quick and easy." I pray that I will leave a legacy for others that will do what is right regardless of the outcome. As for the trial, it is in God's hands! Thank you for serving our community with honor.

A few days later the commander showed up in briefing and personally relieved me of duty in front of my men. They were angry and wanted to know what he thought he was doing and why officers who had committed crimes were not treated as I was. He ignored them. I looked him in the eyes and said, "You will not get away with this!" I was scheduled for a presettlement conference on my lawsuit in January 2001.

No settlement was offered; instead I was terminated two months later in March 2001. This storm of hurricane proportions had utterly and relentlessly wiped out my career, and now I stood in the aftermath of its devastation. When I got home, I collapsed in a chair and buried my head in my hands. I was hot with anger, and God received the brunt of it. I fumed, asking God why he said in his word that no weapon formed against me would prosper; it just wasn't true for me. Almost instantly I heard him say in my spirit, "They fired me. I have released you." With tears running down my cheeks I managed to laugh, and I knew I would have to trust him as this chapter in my life ended and that door closed permanently behind me.

Romans 1:28–30 says, "Since they didn't bother to acknowledge God, God quit bothering them and let them run loose. And then all hell broke loose: rampant evil, grabbing and grasping, vicious backstabbing. They made life hell on earth with their envy, wanton killing, bickering, and cheating. Look at them: mean-spirited, venomous, fork-tongued God bashers. Bullies, swaggerers, insufferable windbags! They keep inventing new ways of wrecking lives." I love what God says in Romans 2:3–4. "You didn't think, did you, that just by pointing your finger at others you would distract God from seeing all your misdoings and from coming down on you hard? Or did you think that because he's such a nice God, he'd let you off the hook? Better think this one through from the beginning. God is kind, but he's not soft. In kindness he takes us firmly by the hand and leads us into a radical life-change."

During the arbitration hearing following my termination, I realized that my enemies had used a prayer, a handshake, and the truth to support their claim against me. The two polygraph examiners told the arbitrators that Jessie, the man I had prayed with, was not a credible or reliable witness. He failed to show up to the first test and was forty-five minutes late to the second test. The veteran officer said, "I only tested Jessie on his perception of the truth, and his reality is different from yours and mine." The thirty-year veteran officer told the arbitrator that using an inconclusive rating on the polygraph as evidence against me was not only unethical but unfair. He told them that no board of polygraph examiners would support a test result like mine, and he recommended that I be given another opportunity; his recommendation was denied.

Support came from unexpected places. Ron, the union manager who served as a Narcotics Bureau commander for many years, to my surprise testified on my behalf, saying he had never seen a senior officer (referring to me) treated with such manifest disrespect in his entire career. He challenged the department's use of the informant as a witness against me based on his lengthy arrest record, which included charges for giving false information to the police. Ron pointed out that the department was using Jessie as an agent and had allowed him to enter a secured police facility with six outstanding warrants for his arrest yet had failed to arrest him. Ron also told the arbitrator, a friend of the department's Labor Relations director, that the department was allowing this man to continue to drive on a suspended driver's license in a vehicle that was uninsured, which placed the police in a potentially liable situation.

Other unexpected support came in the form of testimony from my new Lieutenant Tom, who had been transferred six months prior to my termination. Lieutenant Dillon, meanwhile, had been rewarded for his role in initiating the complaint against me and was promoted to captain. Lieutenant Tom told the arbitrators that many other men wanted to testify on my behalf but feared retaliation. He relayed their comments regarding my leadership and integrity and told them, in spite of what the commander and captain had said, it was his opinion that I did not need to be fired for praying with a man. "She has done an outstanding job as a sergeant and has one of the most productive squads at the station," he said. All of this fell on deaf ears, because the decision had been made long before that day.

The final incident used to terminate me revolved around a handshake that occurred on the first day of 2000 at the University Medical Center. I was standing in the emergency room with one of my officers who had been involved in a serious traffic accident while on duty. We had just worked back-to-back twelve-hour shifts, so the men and I were very tired. That fatigue was a contributing factor in the accident when my officer pulled in front of an oncoming car and was broad-sided.

The doctors were working on the officer when the sheriff and undersheriff entered the crowded emergency room and approached me. I acknowledged them with my eyes, and the sheriff bent his six-foot-five body down, pointed his finger in my face, and yelled, "I'm the sheriff. Don't you ignore me!"

I was embarrassed for him and replied, "Yes, sir."

The undersheriff followed, sticking his hand out to me to shake it. The hair on my neck stood up as he said in a sinister voice, "Not ready yet?" To shake this man's hand would have been like shaking Satan's hand and, regardless of the cost, I would not compromise.

The sheriff and undersheriff ordered my lieutenant to write me up for the charge of "Insubordination" because I had failed to shake the undersheriff's hand. My lieutenant complied with their order, and I was administered a written reprimand that was later used to substantiate their claim of "Gross Insubordination."

The truth was spoken to the undersheriff in a letter I wrote to him explaining why I had not shaken his hand. I wrote:

> Dear Undersheriff Dick:
>
> I have struggled with writing this letter to you because of the deep anguish you have caused me and my family. I will never forget your cold callous eyes the day you denied my grievance and the evidence which was maliciously obtained and used against me. You have robbed me of a dream and many years of dedicated and committed service to my community and Department. I remember working for you as a rookie officer when you were my sergeant. I admired your kindness and compassion. So what happened to you? I do not understand why you have such a mean-spirited vengeance against me

Debra Gauthier

when I have done you no harm. In spite of your evil against me I am called to forgive, and I have done that in my heart; my forgiveness does not, however, condone your wicked ways. When our paths crossed in the emergency room on New Year's Day I did not shake your hand out of disobedience, but in obedience to my God. My God makes it clear that I am not to bow down to any other god, and somewhere along the way you have falsely elevated yourself to the status of god. Anyone who does not bow down to you suffers your wrath. Your power is in a pen and your authority has been misused and abused to satisfy your own insatiable appetite for power. As you have judged others, so you too will be judged by the true and living God, and his name is Jesus Christ. Yes, even you will one day bow your knee and confess that he is Lord! God's word says that "pride goes before destruction, and a haughty spirit before a fall," and you are not immune to this law. I am praying that Jesus has mercy on your wicked soul and that he restores and heals those in this department that have been harmed by the strife and confusion you created through your lies and deceit. On the day you fall I will weep, because I was once there.

I sent the letter to him in February 2000 and was not expecting a response. The undersheriff arrogantly continued his intimidation tactics, even attending a service at my church. This man was obsessed to the degree that he would bring his family to my church and sit across from me as he smiled at me menacingly. I also learned he had met with my pastor and told him that I was calling him the antichrist. I could see that that this man was under the influence of dark spiritual forces. Even the officers could see it and were calling him the antichrist. When my own pastor sided with this man I began to understand the power of his manipulation and intimidation.

Around this time I was also experiencing interruptions in my home telephone service. A confidant at the telephone company informed me that my line was being illegally monitored. This informant said the undersheriff was using his wife, who worked at the telephone company, to gain access to my phone line. Proverbs 26:24–26 says that "a malicious man disguises himself with his lips, but in his heart he harbors deceit. Though his speech is charming, do not believe him, for seven abominations fill his heart. His malice may be concealed by deception, but his wickedness will be exposed in the assembly" (NIV). A few months prior to my termination I was notified that the sheriff was awarding several of us with our twenty-year pins. Because of the pain I had suffered at the hands of this man, I had no desire to receive anything from him. I thought, *He can just send my pin to me in the mail.* God, however, had a different plan and began to impress on me to go. I continued to willfully disobey the Spirit's prompting. The day before the recognition event, I was out riding my mountain bike when I asked God to keep me warm because it was a cold and windy day. I was surprised when shortly after my prayer the clouds began to move and the sun came out for the first time that day. I rode the rest of the way cloaked in the warmth of my heavenly Father's love. When I arrived at my truck and finished loading my bike, the clouds moved back in, and it was cold and windy again.

As I quietly drove home, I heard his still-small voice say, "Will you go and accept your pin and shake the sheriff's hand because I love you?" I wept, touched by the love and compassion of my Savior. The question really was, would I trust him? The next day I went to the sheriff's office with several of my academy classmates to receive recognition for twenty years of service. A fellow officer said, "We respected you before, but coming here to get your pin really says a lot about your character!" As I walked into the sheriff's office, I saw the undersheriff and deputy chief who were instrumental in my downfall lurking in the hallway shadows. They said nothing as I walked by but instead they turned and walked away.

In obedience, which is the proper response of our love for God, I stood before the photographer, shaking the hand of the man who had caused this whole devastating event in my life. As I grasped the sheriff's hand, the photographer experienced some sort of technical problem with the camera and told us to hold our positions while he fixed it. So there we were, frozen in this awkward, ironic, unnerving handshake that seemed to last forever. I noticed the sheriff became very uncomfortable and his hand began to sweat. When the photographer finally snapped the picture, the sheriff breathed a sigh of relief, and, letting go of my hand, he said encouragingly, "Hang in there."

"Did he just say to you, hang in there?" a classmate asked.

"Yes, he did," I replied. We both shook our heads in amazement as we walked out together.

Who would have known that my career would end this way, the result of a prayer, a handshake, and the truth? Proverbs 26:24–28 says, "Your enemy shakes hands and greets you like an old friend, all the while conniving against you. When he speaks warmly to you, don't believe him for a minute; he's just waiting for the chance to rip you off. No matter how cunningly he conceals his malice, eventually his evil will be exposed in public. Malice backfires; spite boomerangs. Liars hate their victims; flatterers sabotage trust." Only God could have known and set up this whole thing! Why? Perhaps God sent me ahead of all those who will soon inherit the kingdom of God.

I had a dream during this time. I saw myself carrying my uniform neatly folded, badge resting on top, walking up to the cross where Jesus had died for us. It was still covered in his blood.

With tears running down my cheeks, I knelt down and placed my uniform and badge at the foot of the cross. I was laying down my career, which had become my god, and giving Jesus that place in my heart back to him. I recalled the time Dan and I had been lost in the desert, and I realized that it symbolized the condition of my soul. In John 4, Jesus encounters a Samaritan woman after his disciples had gone to the village to buy food for lunch. In the story, Jesus is resting near a well when the Samaritan woman approaches to draw water, and he asks her for a drink. "The Samaritan woman, taken aback, asked, "How come you, a Jew, are asking me, a Samaritan woman, for a drink?" (Jews in those days wouldn't be caught dead talking to Samaritans.)

"Jesus answered, "If you knew the generosity of God and who I am, you would be asking me for a drink, and I would give you fresh, living water" (9).

Like this woman, I had no concept of my deep thirst or this gift of God. In my experience I had descended to that place called desperation where nothing else will satisfy the deep soul thirst but living water. On that rainy day in August, I met Jesus at my empty well of self-sufficiency and accepted his living water. Proverbs 8:35 tells us, "When you find me, you find life, real life, to say nothing of God's good pleasure. But if you wrong me, you damage your very soul; when you reject me, you're flirting with death."

A few years ago while speaking at a conference; I met Joe, a police officer from Brockton, Massachusetts. After listening to my testimony, he wrote me a letter that touched my broken heart. He wrote:

> I hate to say that I am glad you are speaking out against the injustice in the name of policing and I hope it will open people's eyes to the internal pressure we all experience in our daily jobs. What you shared speaks of the important role that women

play in policing and women such as yourself pave the way for all of us. I have had years just like yours and I find that you have to keep in mind that you are right and that this never should have happened. If police departments want to keep pushing the buttons, people like you have to stand up. Just remember all the men that are watching. If you win, they will cheer; if you lose, they will say what meets the agenda. On behalf of myself and the silent majority of male brother officers, thank you; keep up the fight, it's worth it!

So does God still move storms? I will leave you with His answer in the following story.

On a plane trip to Chicago to visit my nephews and niece, we were forced to land in Denver due to the weather. As we prepared to land, the pilot advised us that Chicago O'Hare Airport was closed due to thunderstorms. I had promised my nephew Bryan that I would make his Little League game that afternoon, and I asked God to move the storm. A few minutes later the flight attendant came on the intercom and announced that we had fifteen minutes to board the plane and fly between the storms.

When we landed in Chicago it was pouring down great sheets of rain, and the whole area was covered in ominous-looking, dark, black clouds. I hurried to passenger pickup and smiled as I saw my niece Taylor, who was six years old, and my ten-year-old nephew Bryan waving their arms frantically to get my attention. Bryan was so excited that I was going to finally get to see him play ball. As the storm raged around us, I asked Bryan if he believed that God could calm the storm. He nodded yes, and Taylor said, "I believe too, Aunt Deb."

We joined hands in the back of the van and praised God for being mighty in power. We thanked him confidently for what he was about to do, making a way for Bryan to play his game by moving the storm. Bryan was so precious when he asked God to bring the rain back after the game because the fields needed to be watered. I am always amazed at the faith of a child. My sister Doreen pulled up to the house, and I ran in to drop off my luggage as Bryan threw on his uniform. It was still raining as we drove to the field, and I looked at Bryan and Taylor and said, "Only believe!"

Moments before arriving at the field, Bryan yelled out, "Look, there is a small hole in the clouds!" The wind began to blow, and the hole became larger and larger until the black clouds had now dissipated and the rain stopped. After we had arrived with the rest of the team, the wind continued to blow, which dried off the field. The boys began to warm up and the coach informed us the field was in good condition and ready for the game. By the time the umpire yelled, "Let's play ball!" the sky was completely clear, and the sun was now warmly shining on us.

I recalled the story in the Bible where Jesus rebuked the wind and told the waves to be still during a storm that the disciples thought would overtake them. This was the same God, and I was amazed that he would take the time to show up at a little league game to make a young boy's dream a reality. Bryan shared what had happened with his teammates and they asked him if God would help them win. Bryan, with rock solid faith, said, "God can do anything!" They won the game twelve to zero, a shut-out and their first win of the season after suffering five losses.

As we gleefully walked back to the van after the game, as if on cue, the dark black storm clouds quickly returned, and the thunder roared in the background. I told the kids that God was showing off and they laughed. We drove off as rain began to fall again, and Bryan thanked God for watering the earth and giving the animals a drink. God smiled!

Debra Gauthier

I do not know why God sometimes chooses to move the storm and other times he will lead us through the storms in life. All I know is that he is faithful to do what is best for us and his purpose in our lives. I learned from my niece and nephew that approaching these challenging times in our lives with childlike faith is the answer to maintaining our peace. When we respond that way...God smiles!

Look and See

I look to the sky and what do I see?
I see you smiling down on me.
I look to the mountains and what do I see?
I see your walls protecting me.
I look to the valley and what do I see?
I see your light guiding me.
I look to the plants and what do I see?
I see your love for me.
I look to your Word and what do I see?
I see Your Son who died for me.

Poem I wrote on February 22, 2002

"Mom, Are You Sitting Down? I'm Gay!"

God rescued us from dead-end alleys and dark dungeons. He's set us up in the kingdom of the Son he loves so much, the Son who got us out of the pit we were in, got rid of the sins, we were doomed to keep repeating.

Colossians 1:13–14

One evening I was watching a news broadcast where a boy had entered a flood channel during a rain storm and was quickly swept away. The camera crew filmed the boy bobbing up and down in the current, and I watched as a police officer was lowered from a bridge in an attempt to rescue the boy. As the boy rushed by in the tumultuous waves, the officer reached down to grab him, but the water was too powerful and he lost his grip. The helpless boy continued down the channel and disappeared as he was swept under at the channel's end. We watched in silence as his lifeless body was later removed by rescuers. I did not realize then that this event was mirrored in my own life as I was swept down a channel of a sin that would lead to my destruction had it not been for my rescuer.

I unknowingly approached the flood channel of my life during my teenage years when I began to be attracted to other girls. It was a confusing time for me, and although I tried to date boys, I had difficulty relating to them. When a boy would try to get close to me it would cause a deep fear. The fear caused more confusion and uneasiness as I tried to find my way through these experiences. I knew something wasn't right, but I had no idea what to do about it. I was afraid of being labeled a lesbian, which drove me deeper into isolation and a denial of my struggle. I remember spending the night with my best friend, Alice, during my high school years and being tormented by feelings I had for her. We would often sleep together, and I would fantasize about her, being careful not to alert her to my desires. I began to believe I was a homosexual and that my struggle would end when I finally accepted that fact.

I stepped fully into that dangerous flood channel when I was seventeen years old. I was playing softball in a summer league that was coached by a woman named Candy. She had played semiprofessional softball in the Midwest and had moved to Las Vegas with her lover, Susan. They were several years older than me; their close relationship intrigued me. Susan often commented on my physique and touched me in a way that made me very uncomfortable. I rode to practice on my bicycle, and Susan would yell out that my seat fit me well. She laughed at my embarrassment, and my teammates would tease me, saying, "The coach's girlfriend likes you!" This only added to my self-consciousness and confusion.

One afternoon it began to rain, and the practice was cut short. I had ridden my bike to practice, so the coach offered to give me a ride home. Candy and Susan loaded my bike into their van, and on the way to my house, they introduced me to a side of my sexuality I had never experienced before. It was all new to me. I was scared but curious, and I chose to go along with their advances. When I got home that night I felt a loss of innocence, and I knew something had changed in me. Unknowingly I was now being swept down that flood channel toward destruction.

I continued to play sports in college and was further exposed to homosexuality through the coaches and players. The camaraderie and friendships often progressed into sexual encounters, and I felt myself being pulled deeper and deeper into it. As with the boy in the flood channel, the current was too strong to resist, and I found myself being swept downstream. I befriended a girl on my softball team named Wendy. We began to spend a lot of time together studying, playing ball, and socializing. Our friendship grew closer over the months, and before long we both were struggling with physical desires toward each other.

One night we were out drinking with some friends, and I ended up kissing Wendy. Before long we were making out in the back bedroom while everyone else partied. We became an item within our circle of friends, and this became my first dating relationship with a woman. After graduating from college, Wendy went on to medical school, and it was the last time I would see her. Shortly thereafter, I joined the police department, and my life dramatically changed.

The law enforcement career field gave me many opportunities to meet other women who were in the gay lifestyle. The more I associated with them, the more comfortable I grew with this way of life. Since law enforcement is a boys' club, the women who began joining the ranks formed a group called the Big Girls Club. The companionship we enjoyed evolved into sexual relationships among many of the women. I was attracted to one of the women in particular who had just joined, and it wasn't long before I got involved with her sexually. I felt a sense of belonging I had never experienced before. I felt safe and comfortable with these women.

When I was twenty-one years old I decided to come out of the closet with my homosexuality; my mother would be my first confidante. One day while chatting with her at her workplace, she noticed the ring I wore on my left finger and asked what it was. I knew it was time to tell my mother about my hidden life. I took a deep breath and told her it was a friendship ring from the woman I was in relationship with. My Roman Catholic mother immediately grew angry and asked what that meant. I told her I was gay and that God made me that way and he still loved me. It was finally out, and I saw the shock and horror on my mother's face as she fought back tears. All she could say was that God did not make me that way and that I was going to miss out on his plan for my life.

I didn't realize the truth that my mother had spoken nor that her anger was not toward me but toward the sin I was choosing to live in. Over time we grew further and further apart as I went deeper into the homosexual culture. Seeing my mother and family only during the holidays became the pattern, and an awkward tension always hung in the air when I brought my girlfriends home. My two brothers grew very distant, and my sister refused to acknowledge my relationships. It was easier for everyone to pretend nothing was wrong, even though I knew they harbored resentment toward me.

The enemy used my childhood in a violent home with an alcoholic father and an emotionally detached mother to deceive me about my sexuality. The traumatic events in my life led me to develop a wrong pattern of thinking that men were not safe, causing me to fear them. I used that wrong thinking to justify my behavior and later bought into the feminist movement, which fueled hatred toward men. I had no idea that wrong thinking would become a stronghold in my life that would lock in the pain from my childhood and lock God out.

In the early 1980s it was difficult being in public because the lifestyle was not accepted. When others were around, we would pretend to be close friends and refrain from any outward expression of affection. I hid my embarrassment and shame behind a mask and rationalized my feelings by blaming the world for

Debra Gauthier

not accepting me for who I was. This only reinforced the isolation and separation I was feeling and drove me further into the homosexual culture.

My second relationship lasted for about five years, but I soon grew dissatisfied and moved on to other women. Before long I was sleeping around with several women and always looking for a new adventure. The bar scene and the new acceptance of homosexuality made meeting other women much easier, and our relationships became more open. I began to attend the Gay Pride events in different cities and meet women from all over the country. We would often meet on gay cruises and vacation together.

I remember one year flying to Miami to board a lesbian-sponsored cruise ship to the Caribbean Islands. I was going that year with Anita, a friend of mine who asked me if I would go with her to Pennsylvania to visit her family en route to Florida. I agreed, and after spending one day with her family, I was completely bored and began getting restless. Anita phoned a couple she knew in Pittsburg and asked if they would put me up for a couple days while she visited with her family. They were happy to have me as their guest and agreed to meet halfway.

When Anita told me she had made arrangements for me to stay with this couple, I was amused until she told me Norma would be picking me up. The name Norma conjured up a picture of this homely woman wearing a ratty old housecoat, slippers, and rollers in her hair. I was trying to imagine what this experience would be like when we pulled off the freeway and Anita waved at her friend Norma—quite the opposite of my imagination; she was a beautiful Italian wearing cutoff blue jeans and driving a convertible BMW. My mouth dropped open, and I said, "Is that Norma?" Anita just smiled and said she knew I would like her. I grabbed my suitcase, not wanting to look too eager, and climbed into Norma's convertible. It wasn't long before we were laughing and getting to know each other.

When we got to Norma's house, she introduced me to her long-time lover, Corrine, a very attractive woman with short, jet-black hair and deep green eyes. Corrine ran her own personal training business in addition to her job with FedEx. Norma and Corrine took me to dinner and then out to the clubs to meet other lesbians in their community. It was two days of bliss, and I later had an affair with Norma; Anita had a hard time getting me to leave. Once I had stepped into the gay lifestyle, there were no boundaries anymore, so sleeping around with other women—whether they were in a relationship or not—was really no problem for anyone.

I was not yet "out" at work—that is, not until I met a woman named Andrea while I was teaching at the police academy. I learned she had met me a year prior when she saw my picture and an article in the local newspaper about me being the first female sergeant overseeing the police academy. She later told me that she used to listen to me on the scanner and then go out with her husband to drive by my location. She told her husband that she was going to meet me one day, and a year later she not only met me, but she left her husband to do it. Andrea was selected to go to the police academy and joined several other homosexual women whose style was much more militant in appearance. All of them had their hair cut into military flattops, but Andrea wore hers spiked with yellow highlights.

While I taught at the front of the class, I noticed Andrea staring at me the entire time. When the class graduated, the Big Girls Club hosted a party for the new women recruits, and I met Andrea. There was something about her that was alluring, but I often felt manipulated and controlled by her. The relationship was more lust than love, and it took me to a deeper level of darkness as we became more heavily involved in pornography.

After a year together, Andrea asked me to marry her, and we set a date. We commemorated the union at a local gay church.

I invited my mother, but she refused to come, which did not surprise me. Our ceremony was led by a gay male priest and a woman priestess. We lit candles and performed cultic rituals, and I sensed the darkness around us. I had no idea that I had just entered into covenant with Satan and opened my life up to the demonic realm. On the outside it seemed so innocent and pure; Andrea wore a white dress, and I sported a white tuxedo. We cut the cake, shared congratulatory champagne with friends, and then were whisked away in a black limo to our honeymoon—a lesbian-chartered cruise ship to the Mexican Riviera. I had not officially come out at work; however, some of our gay coworkers were invited to the ceremony, so they knew about it. Andrea "outed" me at work because she was very open about our relationship. I, on the other hand, was not comfortable with being out.

I lived in the homosexual lifestyle my entire adult life, so I knew nothing different. I had never been with a man nor had any desire to be with one, so my world was comprised of only women. Andrea and I enjoyed our new committed relationship, but there was always tension between us. Eventually we saw a gay marriage counselor, who told me I was feeling tension because I was not embracing my identity as a lesbian. I did not understand why the more I celebrated my identity and the deeper I got into the lifestyle, the more uneasy I became. Looking back, I knew my involvement with Andrea was dangerous and I had crossed over a line. Our relationship ended after four years when I caught Andrea having an affair with another female officer. I smashed our wedding pictures into pieces and sat on the floor sobbing; it felt as if my heart had been ripped out and stomped on. This only added to the struggle that something was seriously wrong, and I had no idea what it was or how to fix it.

I had gotten involved with the New Age movement and was now delving more into the occult. I experimented with transcendental meditation, astral traveling, psychic readings and rituals, crystals, and anything else that was new and cutting edge. I would often attend New Age conferences put on by different gurus, always hungry to learn more. In my pursuit of spirituality, I became more aware of the demonic realm and began to struggle with fear. I found myself blinded by my own darkness as I opened my soul up more and more to Satan, who masquerades as an angel of light.

As I got deeper into spiritualism, a gift of discerning spirits was activated in me. At the time I was dating Diana, a practicing witch whom I had met at a New Age conference. Diana introduced me to demon worship and a new level of its darkness. One evening as she began to seduce me, my spiritual eyes were opened, and I saw the demon in her sneering back at me. It horrified me! I jumped up, quickly got dressed, and ran out of there. This was the beginning of the blinders coming off my eyes and the exposure of the present dark kingdom of which I was very much a part.

Out of Darkness and into the Light

You groped your way through the murk once, but no longer. You're out in the open now. The bright light of Christ makes your way plain. So no more stumbling around. Get on with it!

Ephesians 5:8–9

When I came out of the darkness into the light, I was no longer able to perform my duties as a police officer with the same callousness as before. When I was born again in the spirit my entire perspective changed. Not only had my world become noticeably brighter but things that would have never bothered me now bothered me. My heart and perspective had changed, and I now looked at humanity with the eyes and compassion of Jesus. I found myself praying for people more often, because many of the problems people faced needed more than I could give them in the natural realm. This change in my police practices would be used against me as my enemies looked for an opportunity to take me out, but God used the persecution to break me so he could remold me into a warrior for his kingdom. I went through a similar breaking and remolding process in the police academy when we were transformed from civilians into police officers. The difference in the process is that man's methods are harsh and destructive, while God's ways are gentle and restorative.

It has been said that you do not come into the kingdom without going through tribulation. We have a choice while we are on the earth; we can humble ourselves during our personal tribulations, asking God to forgive us and receiving his gift of salvation, or we can go through the great tribulation that is coming in the earth where every knee will bow and tongue confess that Jesus is Lord.

I had definitely entered my time of tribulation as everything began to unravel in my world. The investigation against me on the police department was completed, and I not only lost my number one position on the captain's promotional and any chance at becoming a captain, but I was demoted back to a sergeant and placed on graveyard patrol with the call sign 666. When it's your time to come into the kingdom, I believe the enemy knows it and launches an all-out attack to prevent us from coming in. That call sign would be as close as Satan would get in putting his mark on me, and I renounced him and his evil works.

When I returned to work, I called my friend Sergeant Tom, who was our union representative. He immediately had my call sign changed to reflect what my seniority would have been as a sergeant. Instead of 666 my call sign was 509, and I put the stripes back on after being a lieutenant over five years. Although it was a difficult transition, I sensed the Lord's presence, and at some point stopped fighting it, allowing myself to settle into this place where God had me.

While under investigation I spent those work hours when I was ordered to my home reading the Bible. I would spend eight to ten hours per day in the Word. I read the Bible through in just a few short months and immediately picked up another translation and read it through again. I was pretty much alone at work and had no Christians supporting me. It's funny, but only after I was terminated did I find out there were many Christians that worked with me but were afraid to associate with me. I was attending a seeker-friendly church at the time, and my pastor told me that I reminded him of the apostle Paul when the believers in his time had a hard time believing he was actually on their side. I was also in a women's home fellowship, where I learned the pure love between women and I was accepted and unconditionally loved by these women.

While out on patrol one day, I noticed a homeless man walking in the middle of the roadway, causing a traffic jam. I circled around the traffic to stop the man as he crossed the street into a parking lot. He had long, disheveled gray hair with a scraggly beard, and wore several layers of filthy clothing to cover his emaciated body. He told me he lived in a nearby desert, and I saw evidence of bush and dirt on his clothes and hair. I asked him if he had met the Savior Jesus, and he told me he had given his life to Christ when the Christians came to feed the homeless in his area. I asked him why then was he living like a pauper when he was the son of a King. He stood there for a moment to process what I had said, then grabbed my hand and gently kissed it. He walked away a new man, his head held high. When we experience this new birth, our old sinful self dies and we are given a whole new life in Christ. Like the story of Lazarus in the Bible, we come out of the darkness wearing grave clothes and go through a process to shed that old garment and put on the new. We need other believers to help us get the grave clothes off so we can put on our new nature in Christ.

I read in Oswald Chambers' *My Utmost for His Highest*, "The test of the life of a saint is not success, but faithfulness in human life as it actually is." This was much different than what had been programmed into me when I lived as part of the world. I was taught that success was not about others; it was about achieving goals in spite of others. So here I was contemplating that passage, and I began to understand who this God of mercy and love was through the many people I encountered working as a patrol sergeant.

Early one morning, as I sat quietly enjoying the warm sunshine while my patrol car was being washed, another homeless man walked up to me and asked if he could talk to me. His name was Paul, a white man in his midforties. He was dirty and unshaven. I listened as he told me how the cops kept harassing him every time he walked down the street. I told him I could not help him but offered to pray with him as he asked God to help him.

He shared that he had given his life to Jesus at one of the feed-the-homeless programs sponsored by some Christians. I asked him why he was still wearing his grave clothes if he was now the son of a King. He just looked at me as the knowledge of the truth began to set him free. "If you would realize your new identity in Jesus," I said, "you would not be living the way you are, and the police would no longer be harassing you." I could see the light go on in him, and when he walked away the old man had gone and the new had come in Christ.

As a patrol sergeant, I, along with my squad, was responsible for providing coverage of a given area and reducing crime in that area. A particularly challenging area we had been assigned to was a trailer park known for having the highest number of burglaries, drug trafficking, and disturbance calls. When I responded to the park to assess the situation, I noticed it was cluttered with broken-down cars and abandoned boarded-up trailers—a true reflection of the hopelessness in this area.

I asked the manager if he had any security in the park. The answer to that question was a tall lean man introducing himself as Wayne, the security officer. I looked up at him and said, "You've got some work to do here!" I told him I would assign an officer to the area if he would make a commitment to clean up the park in ninety days. He agreed and shook my hand, and I asked him if he knew the Lord. He smiled and replied, "Yes, ma'am!" I told him God was with him and reminded him that he was placed there to be the light that could not be overtaken by the darkness. "He who is in you is greater than he who is in the world," I said. I could see Wayne's faith increasing as he received the power of the Word.

Within weeks the park looked like a new place. Cars got towed, trailers that were vacant now had renters, trash was removed, and lights were replaced that had been shot out. The calls for police service were dramatically reduced when Wayne, with the help of my officers, arrested the people responsible for drug trafficking, essentially taking back ground from the enemy. As I became friends with Wayne and his wife, Carol, I had the privilege of presenting Wayne (who was now called John Wayne) with a letter of commendation for the great job he'd done cleaning up the park. The recognition and prayer support ignited a fire in Wayne, and he became our eyes and ears on the streets, identifying and gathering intelligence on meth labs and even uncovering a child pornography ring in an adjacent trailer park. He was like a one-man patrol squad, and he truly had a servant's heart.

As the Lord continued to turn what the enemy meant for evil for my good, he began to restore things I had lost during the battle. I had purchased an acre of land in the west where I had planned to build my dream house. I lost the land when I was forced to sell it to pay for the attorney's fees during my legal battle on the police department. One day I was driving home when I heard the spirit of God say, "Your trial has ended. Go find your home in the west." Although this was God's voice, I still wasn't sure I could actually get a house. I had been praying about a new home in the west part of Las Vegas, but my job was still unstable, and my finances were stretched so thin that I thought it wasn't the right time. But who am I to argue with God?

I called my Realtor, a Christian woman who had been praying for me for years, and told her I wanted to put my house on the market that Monday. Betty listed my house, and we went shopping for new houses that Thursday. Betty had researched several possibilities on the west side for us to tour. As we drove on one of the roundabout circular drives, we ended up getting lost. We stopped the car, and I prayed, "God, you know where you want me to live. Take us there, and we will trust you." We began to drive away when we both noticed the sign of a development we had not even considered.

When we walked into the model, I felt the presence of God as I realized the floor plan was exactly like the custom home I had planned to build, right down to the skylights in the study. I began to cry, and Betty shouted, "This is it!" The saleswoman told us that the builder was in closeout and she only had three lots left. We drove to the area and looked at the lots, but I knew it wasn't any of these. The saleswoman said, "Wait a minute. A couple just lost their financing, so their lot is available." We drove up a hill and looked at the one remaining lot next to a park, and I knew that was it.

Back at the sales office, the sales agent wrote up the contract and asked me what upgrades I wanted. The house already cost more than I would have considered spending, but I knew God was in it, so I listed all the upgrades I wanted. Then the saleswoman said, "The builder made a decision this morning to include five-thousand-dollars-worth of upgrades as an incentive to sell the remaining houses." I was amazed at the goodness of God.

As I drove home, I was so touched by the love of this God whom I had met only two years before that I began to cry. I said, "Lord, thank you for what you have done for me, but you know I cannot buy this house without selling my other home." When I arrived home, there was a message on my recorder from a retired couple in Detroit, who said, "Our son-in-law who lives on the next street told us about your home. Don't sell it because we are flying in this weekend to buy it." I started jumping up and down praising Jesus for his goodness.

That weekend my neighbor's parents flew in and bought my house at list price. I had sold my house and purchased a new one in less than seven days! I had one month to move, and I was ecstatic. During that time the Holy Spirit told me it was a new beginning and that I was to take only my clothes and my dogs and was to give all my furniture away as a seed for the new.

I met with a dear Christian sister who had given her couch away to a family in her church who had lost their home in a fire. She shared that she'd argued with God and told him she had just purchased the couch and was in need herself, but she finally gave in and was obedient. The family was overjoyed with the new couch, and Jill's living room was once again bare. So when I told her she was getting brand new living and dining room furniture, with all the accessories, she looked at me in complete surprise.

A few days later Jill came to my house with her beloved, Billy, and loaded the U-haul with my new furniture. As she was driving off, I heard the Holy Spirit tell me to call Wayne and Carol and have them bring their truck because I had some things I was getting rid of before my move. They arrived later that evening, and we stood in my barren living room with my stereo playing in the background. I had asked Wayne and Carol what they liked to do in their leisure time, and they told me they loved to watch movies. Because of their financial position they were not able to go to the movies, and all they had to watch was an old color television that had poor reception.

I turned on my fifty-inch big screen television and put in a videotape as I cranked up the surround sound and watched as Wayne and Carol broke out with the broadest smile. I asked Wayne how he liked the sound, and he responded, "Sarge, this is a little piece of heaven."

I looked over at them and said, "Wayne and Carol, the Lord wants you to have this." They just looked at me with unbelief, and tears welled up in their eyes. I told them that Jesus loved them very much and wanted to bless them more than they could ask, think, or imagine. Carol started jumping up and down praising the Lord while Wayne just stood there in a state of shock.

I helped them load their new big-screen television and stereo system into Wayne's truck, and watched as they drove off beaming with joy. I felt the pleasure of the Father, and I was reminded of the day shortly after I was born again when God asked me if I would be His slave. In Galatians 1:10, the apostle Paul referred to himself as a "servant"—a word sometimes rendered as "bond-servant" but frequently also as "slave." He asked, "Do you think I speak this strongly in order to manipulate crowds? Or curry favor with God? Or get popular applause? If my goal was popularity, I wouldn't bother being Christ's slave."

The term *slave* in the world's system has a negative connotation and signifies the oppression of man. In the kingdom, however, slaves are committed to serve the King, and they do not manage their own lives. People who call themselves slaves of Christ acknowledge that the Savior has power over them. As I considered God's invitation to be His slave, I heard Him say, "I treat my slaves well!" How could I say no? So I said yes, unsure of what that would look like.

When I was ready to move into my new house a few months later, the Lord faithfully provided me with all new furniture. I was amazed at how many times I would go shopping and the store was having a fifty-percent-off sale on the items I needed. Everything I had given away the Lord replaced, and I had more than enough to pay for it. I now was living in the double-blessing zone, knowing that my house was a gift from my Father in heaven. Unlike the world's ways of getting what you can, the way to receive in God's kingdom is to give. The more you give, the more you receive.

Although I experienced many blessings during this time of trial in the police department, I was still facing the battle for my career. It seemed that every motion and every appeal filed by my attorney was overruled, and I was beginning to see the handwriting on the wall. I was also adjusting to my new life as a born-again believer and was still in culture shock. As I began to experience the new kingdom culture, there were two things that my eyes were opened to almost immediately. The first was that I felt a dark cloud lift off of me; everything appeared to be lighter. The second thing I realized was that I had an enemy, and it was not flesh and blood.

I was amazed at how fast all the women I used to be associated with abandoned me once they realized I was no longer the person with whom they were familiar. I was facing the battle of my career, and all my support was gone. There I was, alone and in a foreign place much different than the world I had come out of. I recalled a time in college when I had taken a pottery class. The teacher gave us a large, square piece of clay that was as hard as a rock. The first step of the process was to soak the clay in a bucket of water until it absorbed the liquid and became pliable. Then we placed it on the wheel to be molded into a pot. It was a lot of work, pressing and molding that clay into a vessel. I realized it is the same process we go through when we meet Jesus for the first time. Like clay, we come into the kingdom hardened by sin, and it takes a lot of soaking in God's presence to become pliable enough for him to begin molding us into a vessel worthy of him. Isaiah, the prophet, wrote in 64:8, "Still God, you are our Father. We're the clay and you're our potter: All of us are what you made us." So there I was a rock-hard piece of clay as God began to bathe me in his love and speak kindly to me in his Word. As I read the Bible, it was as if God was gently dipping me in the water to soften my hard heart while the Holy Spirit began exposing the lie I had lived in for my entire adult life. My brother and his wife had given me the New King James Spirit-

Filled Bible, and in the back of it were questions. One of the questions said, what does the Bible say about homosexuality?

The answer: "The Bible says that it is an abomination for a man to lie with a man as with a woman, or a woman to lie with a woman as with a man. The apostle Paul called it "shameful," the result of being given up by God to "vile passions. We are told in the New Testament that those who practice homosexuality will not enter the kingdom of God. The apostle Paul shows homosexuality as a final order of rebellion against God. When people exchange the truth of God for a lie, and begin to worship the creature instead of the Creator, they are given up to evil. When values are turned upside down and moral anarchy appears, men burn with lust for other men and women burn for women, and they will receive in their own bodies the punishment for their actions. From a biblical standpoint, the rise of homosexuality is a sign that a society is in the last stages of decay" (New King James Spirit-filled Bible Spiritual Answers to Hard Questions, pages 2002–3).

When I first opened the Bible and read that passage, the blinders came off my eyes, and for the first time, I realized that homosexuality was sin. Coming out of that depth of darkness is a process, and deliverance often comes in stages. Prior to my encounter with God I had no grid for truth. Like many people in our culture today I believed that people were born gay. When I was faced with the truth in the Word of God it was like a slap in the face. It literally snapped me out of my deception. As far as growing as a Christian, it was like the Holy Spirit put Miracle Grow on me and I grew very fast! I was hungry—no, famished—and very thirsty living all those years in the world without God. It was not until I was forty years old that I met Truth and read the Bible for the first time. I was shocked. I had always justified my sin by saying that I was born that way, right? The Holy Spirit led me back to the beginning. I learned that we were created in the image of God, male and female. There was no mention of homosexual as another species. I also discovered that God created the universe, and it wasn't the result of a Big Bang theory with man having evolved from an ape as I had been taught in school.

For the first time in my life, I was face to face with the truth, and I did not know what to do. I was stirred by the apostle Paul's statement in 1 Corinthians 6:9–10, "Do you not know that the wicked will not inherit the kingdom of God? Do not be deceived: Neither the sexually immoral nor idolaters nor adulterers nor male prostitutes nor homosexual offenders nor thieves nor the greedy nor drunkards nor slanderers nor swindlers will inherit the kingdom of God" (NIV). My heart was pierced as I was faced with a decision that had eternal significance. I was encouraged when I read verse 11 in that same passage, "And that is what some of you were. But you were washed, you were sanctified, you were justified in the name of the Lord Jesus Christ and by the Spirit of our God."

I remember standing in my room, overwhelmed with emotions, and I asked God how I had been so wrong even though it had seemed so right. He led me to the book of Genesis, where I read how the snake had entered the garden and deceived Eve by getting her to doubt God at his word. The snake had done the same thing in my life when he asked, "Did God really say homosexuality is wrong? After all, you were born that way." He had begun to whisper lies when I was a little girl and took the label of "tomboy" and used it against me as a word curse to get me to doubt my sexuality. That led to confusion and eventually hatred toward the feminine aspect of my own gender, which I perceived as weakness. The trauma I had experienced as a little girl was the opening that the snake used to enter my life. Because I was not taught the truth in the Word of God, I was deceived as Eve was and entered into temptation and a lifestyle of deception.

Even though my father and mother chose to live in rebellion, God did not give up on us. He sent Christians like Al and Alice, who opened their home to us and prayed for my family, and Jerry and Joanne, who also took care of us when my mother was away working. They modeled a true Christian family, and their homes were filled with peace and joy. God did not leave me alone.

The Holy Spirit began to reveal to me Satan's craftiness, how he had set up a counterfeit kingdom on the earth, of which I had unknowingly been a part. He showed me that the symbol for gay pride is not by coincidence a rainbow. In Genesis 9:12–13, God continued, "This is the sign of the covenant I am making between me and you and everything living around you and everyone living after you. I'm putting my rainbow in the clouds, a sign of the covenant between me and the Earth." The Holy Spirit further revealed to me when I had participated in the unholy union with Andrea, I had unknowingly entered into a false covenant with Satan, who counterfeits the true—and breaking that connection would not come without a spiritual battle.

In my first month in God's kingdom, I had a visitation in the night. I felt a bone-chilling cold come into my bedroom. I was suddenly paralyzed with fear as I lay on my back, staring at the ceiling. In the reflection of light coming from the window, I watched in horror as a bony hand reached down toward my head. I tried to cry out to Jesus, but nothing came out of my mouth. The hand physically grabbed my hair, and it pulled so hard that my head came up off the pillow. I was frozen with fear when I heard that still, small voice tell me to put on my armor. In my mind I began to put on the armor of God, piece by piece. When the last piece was on, there was a flurry of activity, and I could see shadows moving around my bed. I heard what sounded like wings rustling, and suddenly the demon was gone.

There were other strange occurrences too, like the time I woke up to find my cross necklace lying on the floor next to my bed. It was still clasped, and it was unexplainable how it had been removed from my neck. As a police officer on the streets, I was able to see the enemy I faced in the flesh, so I was not prepared for this type of invisible engagement. I also had to get familiar with new weapons of warfare. I discovered that my carnal weapons were useless in the spiritual realm. Over time I would learn how to take authority over the spirit of fear that was tormenting me.

As the Holy Spirit continued to reveal truth to me, the answer of how I had gotten so deceived was revealed in Romans 1:18–27:

> But God's angry displeasure erupts as acts of human mistrust and wrongdoing and lying accumulate, as people try to put a shroud over truth. But the basic reality of God is plain enough. Open your eyes and there it is! By taking a long and thoughtful look at what God has created, people have always been able to see what their eyes as such can't see: eternal power, for instance, and the mystery of his divine being. So nobody has a good excuse. What happened was this: People knew God perfectly well, but when they didn't treat him like God, refusing to worship him, they trivialized themselves into silliness and confusion so that there was neither sense nor direction left in their lives. They pretended to know it all, but were illiterate regarding life. They traded the glory of God who holds the whole world in his hands for cheap figurines you can buy at any roadside stand.
>
> So God said, in effect, "If that's what you want, that's what you get." It wasn't long before they were living in a pigpen, smeared with filth, filthy inside and out. And all this because they traded the true God for a fake god, and worshiped the god they

made instead of the God who made them–the God we bless, the God who blesses us. Oh, yes!

Worse followed. Refusing to know God, they soon didn't know how to be human either——women didn't know how to be women, men didn't know how to be men. Sexually confused, they abused and defiled one another, women with women, men with men—all lust, no love. And then they paid for it, oh, how they paid for it—emptied of God and love, godless and loveless wretches.

I was shocked as I read this passage and knew it was talking about me. I knew of God but refused to worship him as God, choosing instead to go my own way. The sword of the Word cut me to the core, and I stood guilty of sin and rebelling against the Creator, a Holy God. I would need an advocate to pay the price for my sin, and I gladly received that good news when it was presented to me by the Holy Spirit. Jesus had paid my sin debt, and the slate was swept clean. Wow!

I recalled a dream where I saw a plateau and, standing upon it, a shepherd and a flock of sheep. In horror I watched as the shepherd led his sheep to the edge of the cliff and enticed them to walk off the edge, falling hundreds of feet to their deaths. When the shepherd, who was wearing a hood, turned toward me, I was shocked to be looking into the cold, dark eyes of Satan sinisterly smiling at me. I awoke from the dream in a sweat as I now realized how close I stood to the edge of the cliff, and just who it was I had been following all those years.

Over the weeks that followed, I experienced a godly sorrow over the realization that my identity as a woman and my destiny in God had been stolen from me. I never truly knew the love of a father until I met my Heavenly Father. During a time of devotion, I had a vision and saw in the spirit a scared little girl wearing torn and filthy clothing, walking up to the throne of God. I looked closer and realized that the little girl was me. The Father was standing in front of me with this amazing light emanating from his presence. As this tiny child stood before the glorious Father of lights, I sensed the warmth of his love wash over me. He bent down and gently lifted me into his arms—the safest, most loving place one could ever imagine. I nestled my head in his neck and rested in his peaceful, loving presence. When the Father lowered me to the ground, I was now wearing a glistening white robe and was filled with his awesome healing love that casts out all fear. While standing there, I began to grow into a whole woman of God, free from all the pain and the lies that kept me in bondage for so many years.

One day while hiking in the red rock canyons behind my home, I was worshipping God in his creation and admiring his artistic work, when I heard him say, "My greatest masterpiece was man. I formed him in my image out of the dust of the earth, and then I breathed life into him. I made the woman in my image from the rib of a man in the secret place, and I embraced her, imparting my nurturing spirit into her. I put man in the garden to work it and take care of it."

"Why did you put the snake down here on earth?" I asked the Lord.

I was surprised at his reply: "I desired a family and an army that would one day rule and reign with my Son." The Father had placed man, his treasured creation, right in the middle of the enemy's territory, which pleased him.

It all happened in the garden when the woman engaged in a conversation with the serpent and was ultimately deceived. Genesis 3:1 says, "The serpent was clever, more clever than any wild animal God had made. He spoke to the woman: "Do I understand that God told you not to eat from any tree in the garden?" Like the first woman, I had listened to the snake ask me, "Did God really say you are not gay?" There was a part of me that knew that what I was doing was wrong, but I chose to do it anyway. The Bible calls that rebellion, and I unknowingly lived in that condition for most of my adult life.

I could now see the strategy the enemy had used. He got me to doubt what God said in order to take me captive to his lie. He then set up a series of circumstances that would lead me down a dark path that he had planned for my destruction. In Jeremiah 29:11–14 God tells us, "I know what I'm doing. I have it all planned out—plans to take care of you, not abandon you, plans to give you the future you hope for. When you call on me, when you come and pray to me, I'll listen. When you come looking for me, you'll find me."

Prior to the fall of man in the garden, Adam and Eve were naked and felt no shame. After they fell, they heard the sound of the Lord God as he walked in the garden in the cool of the day. And they hid from him because they were naked and afraid. We all originate from the seed of Adam; consequently we suffer from the shame caused by the sin nature. Only until we are reborn of God do we shed the cloak of guilt and shame and Jesus gives us his righteousness. Colossians 1:13–14 says, "God rescued us from dead-end alleys and dark dungeons. He's set us up in the kingdom of the Son he loves so much, the Son who got us out of the pit we were in, got rid of the sins we were doomed to keep repeating."

After being set free from the shame, I finally called my mother to share what had happened. It had been twenty years since I told her I was gay. Now I came to her with even bigger news. She picked up the phone and I said, "Mom, are you sitting down? I'm not gay! God did not make me that way!" Her reaction took me completely by surprise. She began arguing with me, and told me God loved me even if I was gay. I was shocked to hear my own Roman Catholic mother had also bought the lie of Satan. We talked at length, and I finally convinced her that homosexuality was sin and not part of God's creation.

I called my brother Steve and his wife, Belinda, next and told them I could not be gay and be a Christian. My brother later told me that he cringed, assuming I was going to say I was rejecting Christianity. Instead I said, "I'm not gay. I'm following Jesus!" He began to cry and told me they had placed a prayer request in their church just six months earlier; the whole congregation had been praying for my salvation.

My final call was to my sister Doreen. I told her I had been born again and asked her what I was to do next. She referred me to Central Christian Church, which was an affiliate of the Willow Creek Church she belonged to in Chicago. A few days later I walked into this huge auditorium and watched as the people sang and worshipped God. It wasn't like the Catholic Church I had attended as a little girl. This was much more casual—people wore jeans and shorts—and they looked happy! There was also a genuine love from the people I met. They embraced me, and it was this love that helped me come out of the darkness to begin the healing process.

I signed up for the new believer's class and was baptized a few weeks later as Steve, Belinda, and my mother watched. When I came up out of the water, I felt the power of God all over me, and at that moment my old life was crucified with Christ. My brother and his wife were crying, and we joyfully embraced as part of God's family. When I went to hug my mom, her body stiffened, and she was as cold as ice, just looking at me strangely.

That night while I slept, I felt a breath on my ear as I heard Jesus whisper, "Forever." I immediately awoke, overwhelmed by the presence of God. Later in a dream, I saw Jesus walk up to me as he took me by my hand and placed it on the scars of his hands and feet as he lovingly smiled at me. I awoke from the dream with tears running down my cheeks. The depth of his love is unending, and I was touched by his desire to share what he had suffered for me.

As I began to walk with Jesus, I struggled with a sense of uneasiness when I was in his presence; I knew the fear I had of men was being triggered. I was soon to be delivered from this fear while attending an Exodus Conference in Chicago. I attended a workshop led by Leanne Paine, who ministers to people who are coming out of the homosexual lifestyle. She used visualization as a technique to help in the healing process. Leanne asked us to close our eyes and imagine the garden in our heart. As she began to describe a beautiful garden, I just felt discouraged because I could not see anything. It seemed the harder I tried to imagine this garden, the more frustrated I became. She told us to keep pressing in if we did not see anything, so I tried again and finally I began to see a beautiful garden. It was lush and green with a waterfall and a river running through it. As I walked along a path through the garden, I noticed an ugly dark green plant in the middle. It had jagged leaves, and I knew it did not belong there. I walked over and grabbed the stalk of this plant and began to pull it out. As I pulled, I felt a pulling sensation in the pit of my stomach. The roots were very deep! I pulled harder and harder until it finally broke free, and I fell backwards into a stark white room. "What was that?" I asked. And I heard in my spirit, "That was your fear of intimacy. It is gone!"

Suddenly I was back in the garden walking along the path, but this time I was a little girl. As I walked I saw weeds growing all along the ground. I began to pull them out but realized there were too many, and I began to cry. I looked up and saw Jesus smiling as he walked toward me with a rake on his shoulder. I watched as he raked all the weeds into a big pile. When finished, he walked over to me and said, "That was your fear of men. It is gone!" He then reached out his hand to me, and I knew that in order to be free to share intimacy with him I must take his hand. I stood there staring at his hand for what seemed like a long time. Finally I reached out and he grabbed my hand, and when he did, the chains of that bondage fell off of me. We walked together in the garden of my heart; it was both electric and soothing all at the same time. I felt love filling every broken place in my soul and the electricity of his presence restoring life back into me. Second Corinthians 5:16–17 says, "Because of this decision we don't evaluate people by what they have or how they look. We looked at the Messiah that way once and got it all wrong, as you know. We certainly don't look at him that way anymore. Now we look inside, and what we see is that anyone united with the Messiah gets a fresh start, is created new. The old life is gone; a new life burgeons! Look at it!"

I did not realize just how new I had become until I went back to work. I looked at the men I had worked with for years and asked God, kind of jokingly but seriously too, "What are these?"

"They are men," He replied. "I made them for your mate." I had never even noticed them before, and now I was more comfortable around them and actually found them attractive. I too was different; I looked softer, which the men that I worked with immediately noticed. They asked what had happened to me, and I told them I had met my Savior Jesus and had fallen in love. I also shared that I was not gay, and they were shocked! It wasn't long before the officers began asking me to pray for them and they too were born again.

Forgiveness—the Way of the Cross

In prayer there is a connection between what God does and what you do. You can't get forgiveness from God, for instance, without also forgiving others. If you refuse to do your part, you cut yourself off from God's part.

Matthew 6:14–15

After suffering a two-rank demotion, I filed a lawsuit and fought to be vindicated, but I lost every appeal. My attorney finally called and told me to empty my bank account, because the police department was coming after me for seventy-five thousand dollars in legal fees. I hung up the phone in dismay and wondered where God was during all this. That's when I sensed a presence behind me, and my spiritual eyes opened to see an angel as tall as the ceiling, standing in my living room. In my spirit I heard, "Your attorney told you to empty your account out of fear. I am telling you to empty your account in faith, and give the money to the poor." I had one choice, and that was to obey. So I emptied my account and gave a two thousand dollar check—which was all the money I had left in my savings account—to the benevolence fund at church.

I was constantly being amazed by God's faithfulness. My attorney called me just a few weeks later to tell me the lien for the attorneys' fees had been dropped and I was no longer responsible for them. I continued to experience more of God's restorative power as he began to deal with me about forgiving the men in the police department who had been a part of my downfall. I was about to learn the cost of forgiveness and the debt that had been paid. I did not realize that in my battle against the injustice I had been dealt, a root of bitterness had formed in my heart that was strangling the life of God out of me. The Lord exposed that root in the most unusual way.

I was invited to join my friends Joan and Victor at their church one Sunday morning. As I stood next to my friends, I looked down at a young boy about ten years old seated in front of me. He wore a t-shirt with a picture of a serpent that had a man's face sporting a sinister grin. I began to feel uneasy, and I looked to my right; I was not prepared for what I saw. Standing right across the aisle from me was the undersheriff with a face like stone, looking straight ahead. I grabbed my friend's arm as waves of nausea swept over me and the light in my eyes began to dim. As I was about to faint, I quickly picked up my Bible and left the church. Outside the church, I crouched on the curb while beads of sweat formed on my brow. I gasped for air in an attempt to calm myself. As a police officer, I had never once been overcome with such an overwhelming sense of fear. Now, sitting there, I drank in the fresh air and asked Jesus to help me get home. In my spirit I knew that as long as I refused to forgive these men, I was opening myself up to torment by the enemy. The Holy Spirit led me to the story of Joseph in the Bible. I read how his brothers, who were jealous over a dream he had shared, cast him into a pit, intending to kill him. Instead of death, Joseph was sold into slavery by his own brothers and spent many years as a slave. When things could not get much worse for Joseph, he was then falsely accused by his master's wife and sent to prison for a crime he did not commit.

The parallels in Joseph's situation and my own stood out sharply. I could relate to the deep pain and betrayal he felt at the hands of his brothers. My dream of being a captain on the police department had sparked jealousy in my brother officers, and it was not long until they cast me into a pit of despair. I read how Joseph had to make a decision when he faced his brothers during a famine in the land. Over the years God had his hand on Joseph, who eventually went from the pit to the palace and now served Pharaoh in Egypt. When his brothers came for food, they stood before Joseph starving and fearing for their lives. In Genesis 50:19–20, "Joseph replied, "Don't be afraid. Do I act for God? Don't you see, you planned evil against me but God used those same plans for my good, as what is now being done, the saving of many lives."

Intrigued by the story, I now faced a moment of truth. Would I release these men from the injustice they had done against me and trust God to vindicate me? I wrestled with God on this matter, and finally, after two days, I surrendered it to him. I called my attorney and told her it was over. I dropped the lawsuit and released it all to the God of justice and would trust him for the outcome. My attorney felt the weight lift from her shoulders as she had tried in vain to seek justice in the matter. The Holy Spirit began to reveal to me that forgiveness was not condoning what had been done to me but was releasing these men from my heart so the Lord could deal with them. When I released them from my heart, God asked me to bless them. With tears running down my face, and God's amazing grace, I said, "Lord, forgive them for what they have done."

That simple but very difficult act of faith opened up my heart so that God could begin to heal wounds deep in my soul. God gave me signs of the blessing along the way, and I began to find pennies in my path everywhere I went. One day I asked the Lord, "Why do you give me pennies?" I was surprised by his response when he said, "What is least on the earth is greatest in heaven; your rewards are great!"

I began to understand that forgiveness does have a cost. It cost Jesus his life when He laid it down to pay our sin debt. I would have to lay down my right to seek vengeance and justice. I knew I had to obey God's request to pray for those who had persecuted me. And when I prayed, something amazing happened in my heart. All the anger, bitterness, and resentment I had carried for years began to dissolve, which gave God access to my wounded heart, where he gently applied his healing balm. That was the first level of forgiveness; it was now time for a deeper level.

The Lord began to deal with me about forgiving my father, which brought a flood of memories from my childhood. I thought, *Now you've gone too far, God!* I remembered that day when I was working as a lieutenant on the police department and had received a phone call from the homicide commander. He told me they had my father in custody for murder. He had been living with a woman who had threatened to leave him. So he walked into the bathroom where she was getting ready and put his .357 to her head and pulled the trigger. I told the commander I hadn't seen or heard from my father in over twenty-five years and that I did not know this man. My father was eventually sentenced to life in prison for the brutal murder of his girlfriend during a drunken rage. So how could God possibly expect me to forgive this man?

I wrestled with God for a while until something strange happened at work. Candy, a Christian female officer who had befriended me at work, invited me to a Bible study. At first I said no, but Candy was persistent and I finally agreed. At the first meeting, she introduced me to Tom and his wife, who were leading the group. Tom looked at me kind of strangely and asked if I had a father named George. I was shocked as I nodded yes. Tom told me he was the chaplain at the prison where my dad was housed. He said, "We have been praying for you." Tom told me that my dad had given his life to Jesus and was now ministering to the other inmates. He asked if he could give my dad my address, and before I could say no, I again nodded and I knew my heavenly Dad was pleased.

Just before Christmas I received a card from my dad. It had a picture of the lion and the lamb lying together. Inside the card he'd written:

> Dear Debra,
>
> I've asked God a thousand times for a chance to see you before I die. Now I have the chance, I don't know what to say or even begin to say, except that I do want to see you. I thank God for people like Brother Tom. It's strange how the Lord works. God bless you and I always have loved you. Love, Your father

I wept as I realized that I had not heard my dad tell me he loved me since I was a little girl. Now only God could orchestrate these events such that I would meet a woman at work who happens to go to a home fellowship where the man leading is the chaplain of the prison where my father is serving time. My dad and I began to correspond while I awaited approval to go visit him. My first letter from him reflected the words of a man who had been transformed by God. He wrote:

> Dear Debra,
>
> I was going to wait until we had our visit, but I can't wait. I need to talk now, so here goes. This is the best Christmas that I have had in sixty-four years of living on this earth. Thank God for your letter, picture, and card. I've shared your letter with the staff, inmates, officers; some have cried, and many have renewed their faith. Is God awesome or what?
>
> Six years ago, when I honestly and completely surrendered my life to Jesus Christ and asked him

to forgive me, through repentance I was baptized and felt freedom, peace, and love that only Jesus can give us. I had a pretty good job here, but I had to quit because too much of my old self was surfacing; pride, ego, the need to control. I asked Jesus to guide me and to please humble me. For the last year or so I've been praying for the Lord to strengthen my faith. Guess what? After the support that I have received from people here, and your letter, I've been on cloud nine since Saturday. The Lord has completely renewed my freedom from my self, restored my peace, and filled me with love, and a desire to share this with others.

What I share is that it took me a lifetime and the extreme that I had to reach, and what I try to pound into some thick heads around here is that we don't take the ride to the bottom by ourselves. We hurt so many people along the way, to the point that the only way for forgiveness and healing is through our Lord and Savior Jesus Christ. What I stress at Alcoholics Anonymous meetings is that our ego and pride keep us from receiving the love and freedom of Jesus. Amen.

Debra, I had to come to prison to get out of my own prison and become a free man. I thank God every day for this freedom and that I didn't die the way that I used to be. We seem to only thank the Lord when things are going well, but we also need to be thankful for the bad times. If it weren't for the bad things in our lives some of us would never be brought to our knees, and humbled in order to ask Him to come into our lives. May you be filled with the love and peace of Jesus. Love, Your father

Debra Gauthier

As I read his letter, tears welled up in my eyes. I felt the love from a man who had failed miserably at being a father to me and my siblings. God says that he is a father to the fatherless, so that deep longing for a father was met when I received his Son Jesus as my Savior. God showed me that my dad did not know how to be a father because he did not know him. My dad asked if I would forgive him for his failings and bless him. How could I say no after all God had forgiven me for? I released him from my heart and let go of all the anger, bitterness, and resentment.

One day I received a letter from a man who was serving time with my dad in prison, Richard.

> Dear Debra,
>
> I met your father about five years ago; we worked together. It was impossible for me not to take an instant liking to him and I have been affectionately calling him Dad ever since. He truly is one of the best friends I have ever had. He not only secured a job for me (twice), but he also spoke up for me and got me enrolled in a theology class. I often wondered how I could ever repay him, and this just might be the chance.
>
> Dad, from the time that I met him, always talked about his daughters as the most precious things that ever existed and the heartbreak of being separated from them even tore me apart because I have two sons I haven't seen for seven years. As I am a close friend, he let me read your letters, and I must say, I'm very impressed at your commitment to Christ, and I wish you all of the blessings that could ever come your way, especially with your book.
>
> Dad is so looking forward to your visit; he is like a kid waiting to go to Disneyland. Hopefully, your visiting form will be processed very soon; we're all praying for that! Please don't tell him I wrote to

you as he might take it the wrong way, but I just have to let you know that your commitment to him means everything he ever held dear.

He signed it, "Your brother in Christ, Richard." I was amazed that my dad had finally learned to be a father, and I was thankful God had given him another opportunity to be a father, even if it was in the spirit. My heart was touched as I realized God used not only my dad's prayers but those of other inmates to bring me into his kingdom.

The chaplain arranged for me to visit my dad one Saturday morning, so he picked me up for the drive to the prison about an hour outside of Las Vegas. The drive was tense and silent, only broken by the sight of a beautiful rainbow over the sky. I felt God's presence as I kept my gaze fixed on the rainbow, holding on to his promise.

When we arrived at the prison, we went through check-in and were led into a large visiting room. A guard posted behind a desk in the room's center watched us closely as we entered. The chaplain stood by me with his arm around my shoulder, assuring me it was all right. Finally, a guard led a long line of inmates into the room. They stood against the back wall, wearing their denim blue uniforms. I quickly scanned the line to see if I could recognize my dad after a separation of over twenty-five years. The last inmate in line was a frail-looking man in his late sixties. When our eyes connected, I could see the light of Jesus. I knew this was my father. He smiled as he began to approach me with outstretched arms.

As we embraced he was overcome with the joy of seeing his oldest daughter—the long-awaited answer to his prayers. Tears ran down my face as the wound of abandonment and years of pain were healed and washed away. It was a time of great healing and brought closure to a very dark period in both our lives. Years of counseling could not have accomplished what God did that day when I made the choice to forgive and let go. I recall a walk I took about a year ago where I was pouring out my pain and disappointments to God. Suddenly I heard him say, "On the other side of the pain of the cross is the glory!" Was this the glory that he was talking about?

That day, my dad introduced me to his spiritual son, Richard. He handed me a poem he had written while praying for me in March 2001—the month I was terminated. He titled the poem *Rise.* Here is what Richard wrote:

> You have been greatly wounded
> but now you are healed.
> Rise, child of God—O mighty woman of faith.
> Sing praises to the Lord, give thanks to God.
> The battle has been won.
> Rise, child of God—O mighty woman of faith
> Claim the victory, for the Lord has truly
> Delivered you out of the enemy's hand this day
> Rise, child of God—O mighty woman of faith
> Sing praises to God, give thanks to our Lord.
> He did hear you when you cried
> out after being wounded.
> And He did send to you a helper.
> So be of good cheer.
> Sing praises, give thanks to our Lord
> Rise, valiant one—O child of God.

Tears rolled down my cheeks as I hugged Richard and thanked him for the prayers and words of encouragement. Only God could put it on the hearts of men behind bars to pray for a police officer during her moment of trial. And so I learned the value and gift of forgiveness that day in the prison.

Finally, it was time to forgive my mother so God could heal my mother wound. It happened when I was seventeen years old.

My mother had brought a man named Larry home from the bar where they had met. I was sitting at the kitchen table doing my homework when they walked in. I could smell the alcohol on him. He arrogantly walked over to me and slapped me on the side of the head, making a sarcastic comment about me being a good school girl. A rage rose up in me as I picked up the chair I was sitting in and struck him on the back. He turned toward me, and my mother stepped in between us. It was at that moment she made the cut that would wound me so deeply: She told me if I did not like it around there that I could leave. I was crushed that she would choose this man over her own daughter—an abusive man she had just picked up at a bar. I choked back the tears, packed, and left that night, carrying a bitter pain and resentment with me for many years.

Once again I had to humble myself and choose to forgive my mother, releasing all the anger, bitterness, and resentment from my heart so God could heal me. One afternoon during a visit together, I asked her why she would stay with a man she was not married to who was just like my previous father. Although they had lived together for years, he had a dark side stemming from his involvement with the free masonry. "God gives us free will!" she said. I looked at her with sadness, knowing she had made a choice that day to reject the God of mercy and love. Our relationship was never the same after that.

I remember as I was leaving one day, seeing my mother bound in her prison of pride, and I said to her, "You are right. God gives us free will, and there will always be a man between us. His name is Jesus!" She said nothing; she just looked at me with a cold stare as I left. I would not see my mother again for many years.

God divinely healed my mother wound during a conference in Phoenix. As I walked back to my seat, a woman named Beverly grabbed me and held me like a mother would hug a

Debra Gauthier

daughter. At first I was very uncomfortable until her daughter Kelly said, "She is a mother in the spirit." I closed my eyes and saw Jesus standing next to an open door. He was motioning me to come up. I reluctantly went to him and took his hand. We were immediately transported to a delivery room in a hospital. I stood next to Jesus as a woman was about to give birth. We watched as the Lord walked over and took the doctor's place. When the baby came out, Jesus wrapped it in a white blanket, kissing it gently on the forehead, and the baby fell fast asleep. It was the most beautiful and peaceful thing I had ever seen. Jesus then walked over and handed the baby to me. When I look down, I realized the baby was me and the woman giving birth was my mother. Jesus wrapped his arms around me as I held the baby in my arms, and I immediately felt wholeness go back into my soul. My traumatic childhood had shattered my little soul, and one moment in the arms of Jesus had made me whole again. Beverly said, "The Lord has just sovereignly healed you."

Later that evening as my pastor's wife, Connie, drove me to the airport, she told me the Lord showed her he was giving me back the softness that was stolen from me as a little girl. We left the conference at nine p.m. and arrived at the airport at 9:17 p.m., a drive that usually takes thirty to forty minutes. I wasn't sure what was going on until I realized that my flight was at 9:30 instead of 10:30, as I'd thought. At the check-in counter, the attendant told me the gate was already closed. I told him I had to be on that flight, but he said it was impossible. I knew that nothing is impossible with God, so I asked him to make a phone call. He called someone, and when he hung up, he had a surprised look on his face. He said, "Go to the gate!"

When I arrived at the security checkpoint, the line was extremely long, and I asked the attendant if I could go through. She responded, "If these people don't mind." I didn't even have to ask when the people waved me ahead of them. When I picked up my suitcase, there was a penny next to it—a sign of the blessing. I arrived at the gate, and the door was shut as the plane prepared to back out. I told the attendant that I had to be on that plane. She said that was impossible, and I asked if she could make a phone call. She called the pilot, and he told her to open the door and let me board.

I took my seat next to a little girl and her dad. As soon as I sat down, the little girl tugged on my sleeve and said, "I believe in angels." I thought that was odd until I realized that I was still in the glory realm and children are attuned to the supernatural. The father of the little girl apologized and then began to share that he was going through a divorce. He was bringing his little girl back to Missouri, where his parents lived. I could see his pain, and I asked to pray for him. The young man broke down in tears, and as we prayed, he rededicated his life to Jesus. His little girl and I had a great time talking about angels the rest of the flight.

In the glory, we are not bound by time. Healing just happens. All that is required is a forgiving heart and a desire to be made whole. That weekend, Jesus supernaturally healed me and transformed my shattered soul—wounded as result of living in a fallen world—back to the way God had originally made me. When we walk in the kingdom of God it is like heaven on earth, and it defies the limitations of this natural world. One day soon we will once again walk with God in the cool of the day, and he will live among us on the Earth. What a glorious day that will be. Get ready!

Most Memorable Thanksgiving

Thank God for this gift, his gift. No language can praise it enough!

2 Corinthians 9:15

My first Thanksgiving as a newborn creation in Christ was the most memorable of all. That day began with a battle. First I spilled something in the kitchen as I was getting ready to leave. At the same time, my dogs started fighting and refused to go outside. When I arrived at the police station, my lieutenant vented his frustration and insecurity on me. I finally walked out to my police car, only to find the battery was dead. I was familiar with the enemy's tactics to discourage me when the Lord was going to use me. The attack only encouraged me as I laughed at the enemy and praised my God.

My first stop that day was to the home of a man named Dave who had worked in law enforcement as a corrections officer at a facility in Oregon. As I recall, his wife called the station and told us that her husband was a retired law enforcement officer who had given up on life. She asked if one of our officers would mind stopping by on his break to have coffee with her husband. When I got the request, I decided to go so that my officers would not be tied up. I was greeted by his wife, a small and gentle woman, and then led into another room where a fragile, pale man lay in a hospital bed. The woman introduced me to her husband, Dave, and I could see that his legs were twisted like a pretzel under the blanket draped over him. He wore a catheter. I was told Dave was diagnosed with multiple sclerosis and had been confined to bed for six months. I could see a spirit of death over Dave that stirred me up, so I asked Dave if he believed Jesus could heal him. He told me he didn't believe Jesus wanted to heal him because he had sinned in the past.

I opened up the Bible to the story of Jesus healing the paralytic in Luke 5. When I read verse 23, "Which is simpler: to say 'I forgive your sins,' or to say 'Get up and start walking'?" I looked at Dave and said, "Jesus forgives your sins. Get up." Dave began to wiggle his toes and move his ankles, and finally his whole legs. Although physically weak, Dave strained to sit up and began to move his legs to the edge of the bed. Dave got up! "The people rubbed their eyes, incredulous—and then also gave glory to God. Awestruck, they said, "We've never seen anything like that!" (Luke 5:26).

I went into the bathroom to wash my hands, and the Holy Sprit told me that Dave would need spiritual therapy. Just like someone who goes through physical therapy to recover from an injury, Dave would need to read the healing Scriptures daily. When I shared this with Dave, he agreed to commit to this spiritual therapy and to stand on the truth that he had been healed by Jesus's stripes.

As I left, Dave's wife hugged me and said, "Truly, you are an angel sent to us."

I smiled and replied, "No, just a servant being obedient to the Lord."

As I left their house I was alerted to a foot pursuit that one of my guys was involved in. The officer had spotted a man holding a gun to his head outside some apartments. The man saw the officer and fled on foot and after several blocks was apprehended. My officer told me he had almost shot the man when he refused to drop the gun. This day of Thanksgiving had begun with a murder in front of a bar where a man was shot five times and left lying dead in the middle of the street. The day was filled with calls of violent family disturbances.

During the middle of my shift I stopped by a fellow police officer's home. Her name was Doreen, my sister's name. A couple of years ago this woman had watched in horror as her police officer boyfriend took his duty weapon and shot himself in the head while Doreen stood by. Despite the time since this incident had happened, Doreen was still tender with grief. I shared a story with Doreen of a man who had committed suicide, and she began to cry. I told her only Jesus could set her free from the guilt that she felt. I prayed with Doreen as the Holy Spirit ministered to her broken heart. I could see the Lord transforming Doreen, releasing wounds and restoring her. I left her with a Bible commentated by TD Jakes, titled, *Woman, Thou Art Loosed.* With tears in her eyes, she promised to read it.

My shift finally ended after ten long hours. I walked into the locker room to change and was met by a woman named Jackie. She was a new recruit being trained out of my station. She said, "You're the one who has been writing the scriptures on the board, aren't you?" I nodded, reminded that the Holy Spirit had prompted me to write Scripture on the board each day. Jackie's eyes filled with tears as she shared that she was also a Christian and under tremendous pressure to resign. When her discouragement was more than she could bear, she suddenly noticed the words of God written on the board, and she knew she was not alone in this dark place. Those words and our meeting gave her the strength and courage to continue in her training as a police officer. We joined hands and prayed, giving glory to God and praising him for his faithfulness.

As I pulled up to my mother's house, I saw my brother Joe standing in the driveway with a look of anguish. Joe had lived his life away from the family, bound in the chains of methamphetamine. We embraced as we had done many times in the past, but something was different about him now. That false shield of pride was gone, and he began weeping as the struggles he was going through began to spill out. I listened as he shared the pain of not being able to visit his twelve-year-old daughter Jessica because he had lost his visitation rights after his divorce. On top of that, he had injured his knee at work, which was going to require surgery, and he had recently lost his job. He was going through a lot.

As I looked at him with compassion, I could see a man who had come to the end of his self-sufficiency. The years of drug abuse and drinking had taken a physical toll on his body. I could see by the leathered skin and deep lines in his face, which made him look much older than his age that he was tired and had given up. We walked inside together and met with the other members of my family. After dinner we prayed and led my brother Joe in a prayer of repentance, and he asked Jesus to be his Savior. In a moment, Joe was transformed out of the darkness and became my newborn brother in the Lord. At the end of the prayer, he wiped his tears away and we could see the miracle that had just taken place. Peace washed over his sin-strained face and his eyes radiated with the Light and life in them. My brother was now a free man for the first time in his life. My brother Steve, in tears, looked to me and said, "One left," referring to my mother, who was still bound by a religious spirit and hardened heart.

The following day my Christian sister Debbie and I visited my brother to encourage him in his new walk with the Lord. For as long as I could remember, Joe had worn his hair long as a sign of his rebellion. Now he was a new man, so Debbie offered to cut his hair as a sign of his new life in Christ. Joe embraced the symbolic act. With each snip that Debbie made, the long hair dropped to the floor, representing the old, dead life. Now my brother would begin a whole new life with Jesus and a sharp new haircut. We blessed him with groceries to feed his body and a Bible, which would become his spiritual food. My heavenly Father had once again adopted another one of the fatherless out of the world.

Now that the bondage of homosexuality had been broken in my life, I knew it was time to ask the women I had been in relationship with for years to forgive me. God set up an opportunity to do just that in the most unusual way. It happened about a year after I was born again when I received an invitation for the annual Lesbian Super Bowl party, an event I had attended for years. I knew there would be hundreds of women from my past at this event, and I asked the Lord if he wanted me to go. I was surprised when he said, "Go, and be my witness!"

I called my friend Judy, the only lesbian I still had contact with, and told her I wanted to go to the party. She was surprised and said she would go with me so no one would bother me. When we walked into the party, the women stopped and stared at me as if they were seeing a ghost. We went inside to the main room, where a large crowd of women were gathered, and found a seat in the corner. Judy went to get us something to drink, and I noticed many women looking my way and whispering among themselves. Before long they began to come around me. One of the women I had been friends with for years finally asked, "What happened to you? We were your family." I could hear the pain in her voice, and I saw the sadness in the faces of these woman I had known for years.

After a long silence I asked them, "Have you ever fallen in love?" They looked at me with wide eyes and said yes. I continued, "Remember how you spent all your time with that person and neglected all your friends and family?" They nodded their heads yes. I then asked them to forgive me for neglecting them. I said, "I fell in love!"

They now looked at me with excitement and asked, "Who is she?"

"It's not a woman," I replied. They looked like I had knocked the wind out of them as they gasped, "It's a man?"

"Yes," I said, "and his name is Jesus…he swept me off my feet!" At that point you could have heard a pin drop. I looked at several of the women who now had tears in their eyes, and I knew that Jesus was touching their hearts. I left shortly after that, as I knew I had just a short window of time to be his witness.

Forgiveness cost Jesus his life. When I received his forgiveness, I gained his life—a life that I had lost when I chose to live my life separate from God the Father. Because he could not bear spending eternity without us, the Father sent his one and only son, Jesus, to this world to pay our sin debt. When we consider Jesus's great sacrifice and brutal death suddenly forgiveness is no longer a hard thing to do. Maybe there is someone that you need to forgive. Go ahead and release them and watch God do a miracle in your life!

Debra Gauthier

Wilderness—the Place of Surrender

Today, please listen; don't turn a deaf ear as in "the bitter uprising," that time of wilderness testing!

Hebrews 3:8

On September 11, 2001, I stood in my living room watching in horror as the planes struck the twin towers of the World Trade Center in New York City. Their collapse sent a wall of dust and debris billowing throughout the city streets. As tears rolled down my face, I realized that my career was much like those towers that had also been hit by the enemy. I now stood in my own heap of dust and debris as my termination became effective the same year that evil hit our nation.

After my termination from the police department, the Lord led me to the wilderness. In the Bible, the Israelites were God's people who were enslaved in Egypt by the pharaoh, an evil ruler during that time. God led them out of enslavement in Egypt through a man named Moses, and into the wilderness, where they would learn to trust God to protect and provide for them. In a contemporary spiritual parallel, Egypt represents the world we live in; the pharaoh of our day is Satan, a high angel who was kicked out of heaven because of pride. We are slaves of his kingdom until we are spiritually delivered and translated into the kingdom of God when we accept Jesus as Lord. Then we live in the world in right standing with God in the kingdom, which is a place of peace and joy right in the midst of this fallen world.

As a police officer, I had been my own protector and provider, the god of my world. Surrender meant defeat. During my training as a police officer, I was taught that I should never surrender but fight to the death. So here I was in this dilemma: God wanted me to surrender control of my life and make him Lord. Not so easy. Because of the deep wounds I'd experienced in my childhood, I feared not being in control, which felt unsafe. I had to pull down that stronghold in my mind to receive the truth that surrender was the only safe place to be, and it was a place of rest for my soul. I would like to tell you I bowed my knee immediately, but that was not the case. These were difficult times, and I was amazed at God's patience.

On a mild January morning I headed out to the canyons to ride my mountain bike, still angry at God for allowing the enemy to steal my career. As I began to relax into the ride, the Lord began to speak to me. I stopped to write as he spoke the following to me:

> You have to choose to let me reign in your life and do things my way. I *am* the Lord your God. Your anger has a place; I created that emotion. It must be controlled and directed properly. You must learn to yield. If you fail to yield, it is like driving, and you will suffer a crash. Yielding is for your protection. I see things that you do not. You must trust me. My word will not return to me void. Be still and know that I *am* God! I will strengthen and sustain you through this. Trust me and stop fighting. I love you, and I know what you are going through. I went through the same thing in the garden of Gethsemane when I chose to surrender my will and regain what Adam had lost in the garden of Eden.
>
> Now, about love; it is power in my kingdom; it is not necessarily an emotion. When you walk in

Debra Gauthier

love you are doing warfare. If you could see it in the spiritual realm, it literally disables the devil and his demons. Love causes confusion and the demons attack each other. Walking in love is forgiveness, mercy, kindness, gentleness, patience, doing good for evil, blessing your enemies. It gives the angels free reign to work on your behalf. Hate, offense, and unforgiveness give the kingdom of darkness free access to torment and harass you. If you could see it with your spiritual eyes, the demons actually feed off that dark energy in your heart, much like a tick sucking the blood from its host. You must choose to walk in love and not give up!

Now, about the supernatural; Satan wants you to fear it because he knows that once you move into that realm, his reign on your life is over. You will be cloaked in humility, and it will be like chasing a reflection of me to the demons. When you learn to operate in this realm, you will witness signs, wonders, and miracles. The reason the enemy is fighting you so hard is because he knows this is your time of the cross and you are about to ascend to this new level. It is not by might nor by power, but by my spirit. You will go places and do damage to the enemy's camp; captives will go free and many will join you in my kingdom. This realm and revelation only come through surrender. No man will ever boast or get the glory. There is no room for doubt, unbelief, fear, or rebellion. The path is narrow, and very few make it from here.

Now about tears, self-pity, and complaining: I am not moved by any of these things. I am moved by your faith and obedience. Your tears are good for you. They soften the hard ground of your heart and cleanse the body of pain. I will not speak to a hard heart or compete with your flesh. The key to all of this is that I must become more and you must become less.

You will begin to develop supernatural sight and hearing; as you become quiet in your soul, your spirit takes over and you will soar to new heights with my spirit guiding you. Your body is a vessel. You must discipline, train, and feed it the things I created, and then you will walk in divine health if you heed my commands. When the pestilence breaks out in the world it will not affect you. You will have supernatural protection and will trample on snakes and scorpions. Nothing will harm you, but you must abide in me. Stay under the shadow of my wings!

You will speak more in the spirit and not be prone to the voice and lies of the enemy. He is the prince of the air, the ruler of the world. You are not of this world. He works through illusion and deception. When you get this, you will move through the door of the supernatural. This is why you feel like you are drowning. This is entering in; yield, breathe, relax.

The youth are not afraid of the supernatural. That is why I will use them mightily in the end times. Adults want to analyze and understand it before they will go. The natural mind cannot fathom it. It is done by faith, not by sight. The angels and demons already operate in this realm, and it is possible for a reborn human who is willing to let go. It is like when you jumped from the plane. You went with man's assistance and out of fear. This time you will jump through submission and faith.

The revelation I am giving you is what I gave the apostle Paul and John. Paul entered in and walked out of prison, shook a poisonous snake from his hand, and witnessed a revival of healing. John walked in it and received the book of Revelation. Phillip was transported physically in his body to another place when he entered in. Now you will walk in it and accomplish things supernaturally. No eye has seen or ear has heard what I am about to do on the earth. Get excited! I have overcome the world, and you will experience this by walking outside the natural realm.

I was amazed that God would speak to me and in my own language so that I had understanding. I knew there was more than what I had seen of Christianity, and I wanted to walk in that realm with Jesus, which appealed to my sense of adventure. I wanted it all, and he told me I could have as much as I was willing to surrender to him. If I wanted it all, I would have to surrender it all! Was I willing? That was the question.

I remember being on a walk one day when I heard the Lord say, "Be my slave."

I was shocked and said, "I don't understand, Lord. You set me free from being a slave, and now you want me to be your slave?"

He replied, "I treat my slaves well!" I had no idea what I was saying yes to, but it sounded good to me, so I said, "Yes, Lord!" There is a death to self that must take place in the wilderness. In Psalm 116:15 God says, "Precious in the sight of the Lord is the death of his saints." Could this be the death he was talking about?

During my time in the wilderness I went through that dark journey of the soul that happens during the transition from the old nature to the new creation we become in Christ. Even though our spirit is instantly reborn when we make Jesus Lord, our soul has to be regenerated through the process of renewing our minds and aligning ourselves with the truth in God's Word. Since my whole life was built on a foundation of lies, God had to send his angelic wrecking crew to help me tear down the old structure while imploding the foundation.

Because I had lived in homosexuality my entire adult life, I went through an intense battle to be set free from this lie. The apostle Paul talks about this struggle in Romans 7:15–20 when he says, "Yes, I'm full of myself—after all, I've spent a long time in sin's prison. What I don't understand about myself is that I decide one way, but then I act another, doing things I absolutely despise. So if I can't be trusted to figure out what is best for myself and then do it, it becomes obvious that God's command is necessary."

The only way out of homosexuality is through Jesus Christ. I came to the realization that this is the only sin on earth that has become an identity! Think about it. Heterosexuals who have sex outside of marriage are not born as fornicators to justify their behavior, nor are people caught in adultery identified as an adulterer by birth—that is ludicrous. So why is it that people having sex with their own gender are said to have an "alternative lifestyle" and have their own special rights? Could it be that we are seeing the fulfillment of Scripture in 2 Thessalonians 2:11–12? "And since they're so obsessed with evil, God rubs their noses in it—gives them what they want. Since they refuse to trust truth, they're banished to their chosen world of lies and illusions." I had battled the demonic realm when I was delivered from this delusion. I humbled myself and accepted the truth that it was sin and I needed to repent. It was the most difficult battle I had ever faced. The rebellion I fought in my own soul when I surrendered myself to this lie was intense.

As these dark emotions pressured me, I exploded in anger and told God He could no longer have my life. I went into my home office, opened the desk drawer, and pulled out my .9mm

Debra Gauthier

semi-automatic pistol. I took the gun out of the holster, put it to my head, and went to pull the trigger, but it was frozen. I released the magazine and dry-fired the weapon, and the trigger worked fine. I angrily reloaded the magazine and pulled the slide back, loading a bullet into the chamber, and once again put the gun to my head. I pulled the trigger, and it froze again. I went through this process over and over again, and each time the gun worked fine when I emptied it of bullets. I kept doing this, growing more and more frustrated until I heard the Holy Spirit say, "You cannot destroy what does not belong to you! You are not your own. You belong to me!"

I put the gun down and fell to my knees in the presence of a holy God. When I heard a knock on my front door, I answered the door, and my two dear Christian sisters stood there and said, "The Lord told us to check on you. Are you all right?" I invited them in, and as they walked past my office, they saw the gun lying on the rug. They began to pray over me and break the demonic assignment intended to destroy my life. The tears finally flowed, and when it was all over, the battle of surrender had ended, the demons left and God had won!

I have never been married, but I would imagine this was like going through a very difficult time in your marriage, finally having a breakthrough and experiencing a new level of intimacy in your relationship. It was the same thing with Jesus, and now I was free to receive his amazing love! The lack of surrender had been hindering me from entering into deeper levels of intimacy. I had been having difficulty in my relationship with God because he chooses to express himself as a man. I had never surrendered myself to any man, let alone the Son of man. This was a miracle in my life! As I fell deeper in love with Jesus, the lover of my soul, I wrote the following poem.

He set me free.

JESUS is His name.
He healed my broken heart.
JESUS is His name.
He restored my life.
JESUS is His name.
He loves me more than I could imagine.
JESUS is His name.
You are Jesus, God's dear Son,
and his anointed One.
You came to earth humble and
meek to serve mankind.
You taught us things we did not
know and healed our broken hearts.
Demons fled dreading the day of your return.
Many wept when you left and soon
will rejoice when the trumpet sounds.
I am but a stranger on this earth heaven bound.
A soldier taking ground, my
weapon is your Word.
My protection is trust and faith
which shields me from enemy fire.
Take me where you are, Lord.
Lift me to your place of glory that
I might stare upon your beauty.
To touch you, that is what I long for.
To know you as my most intimate friend.
My desire is for more of you,
nothing else will do.
Come, Lord, and fill me up
until my cup overflows.
Break through my heart and con-
sume me with your fire.
It was your love for me that led you there.
It was your love for me that sustained you.
It was your love for me that brought you here.

Debra Gauthier

It is your love for me that will bring you back.
You spoke and your voice boomed.
I trembled in your holy presence, so
small, so vulnerable, at your mercy.
When I was but a little girl
I often thought of you.
Who is this God, I asked.
I walked and talked with you.
You were my friend.
I did not know your name, only
your comforting presence.
I saw you on the cross and my heart cried out.
Why had they done this to you?
It took forty years to understand
the love that you have for me.
O Lord, how glorious is your name. My
rock in which I stand; my deliverer.
The canyons echo your glory; the
mountain tops proclaim your name.
JESUS, the soon coming king!
Let the whole earth rejoice!

Psalm 139:13 says, "Oh yes, you shaped me first inside, then out; you formed me in my mother's womb." Living in deception and sin for so many years had completely unraveled what God had formed in my mother's womb. But the Holy Spirit reformed me and revealed to me who I was created to be. God in his extravagant love and mercy restored the good memories from my childhood that the enemy had stolen. God promises us in Joel 2:25–26, "I'll make up for the years of the locust, the great locust devastation—Locusts savage, locusts deadly, fierce locusts, locusts of doom. That great locust invasion I sent your way. You'll eat your fill of good food. You'll be full of praises to your God, The God who has set you back on your heels in wonder. Never again will my people be despised."

One night I entered into a vision of a windswept beach and saw myself walking along this isolated stretch of sand along the water's edge. Suddenly I heard a sound. It was like no sound on the earth. It was the sound of many waters. As I looked behind me, there was Jesus in all his majesty riding on a white horse toward me. My heart pounded with anticipation as he rode up and extended his hand, lifting me up onto his horse. We rode off, my arms tightly wrapped around the waist of my Rescuer. My cheek pressed against his back as I listened to his heart of love beating for the nations. It was in that place that I heard him say, "I *am* your Prince Charming!"

As I stood up wiping the tears from my cheeks, I noticed that I was no longer wearing the false armor of protection. Instead I wore a robe of righteousness, and I was fully restored as a woman. Like God, I looked at what He had created and said, "It is very good!" Say this: "God you're my refuge. I trust in you and I'm safe! That's right—he rescues you from hidden traps, shields you from deadly hazards. His huge outstretched arms protect you—under them you're perfectly safe; his arms fend off all harm" (Psalm 91:2–4).

Debra Gauthier

Promised Land—
"God, There Are
Giants Out There!"

> Now get yourselves ready. I'm sending my Angel
> ahead of you to guard you in your travels, to lead
> you to the place that I've prepared.
>
> Exodus 23:20

During my journey I crossed over from the wilderness into the promise land, a place spiritually where we face our giants and take back the ground in our souls that the enemy has stolen. The wilderness is a place of rest and intimacy with Jesus, whereas the promise land is a place of battle where we are trained to become kingdom warriors.

I was working in outside business-to-business sales, and the Holy Spirit was using it to teach me things about the kingdom. I learned that my calling in the marketplace was that of a sales evangelist. One day I called on a new client, an exterminator company, and as I waited in their lobby I noticed the atmosphere was heavy and very dark. As I sat observing in the spirit, I noticed a large poster with pictures of insects and words in bold, black letters: *Know Your Enemy*. I began to pray in the spirit and bind demonic forces as I quietly waited to meet with the owners.

An Iranian couple came out, and the man introduced himself as Al and his wife as Rosa. They invited me into their office, where I presented my product and closed the sale. As I walked out to my car, Rosa followed me and asked me if I could help her.

She told me I was different and she liked my energy and wanted to share something that had happened to her that she couldn't talk about with anyone else. I agreed to join her for coffee at her home the next morning. As I drove away I was reminded of the scripture in Isaiah 9:2 that says, "The people living in darkness have seen a great light; on those living in the land of the shadow of death a light has dawned."

I met Rosa at her home early the next morning and walked into a beautiful place on the side of a hill overlooking the valley. Her home immediately filled my senses with the aroma of food that Rosa was cooking from her homeland. As we drank our tea, Rosa began to tell me about her experience. Several months ago as she slept next to Al, a blinding white light illuminated their bedroom. Rosa woke Al and asked him what it was. Half asleep, he groggily replied, "It's probably a police helicopter light; go back to sleep."

Rosa got up and went outside on the balcony and immediately felt the presence of god. She told god that she was not going to leave until he showed her a sign. As Rosa continued to wait, her attention was drawn to a cloud in the sky that was strangely backlit. She watched as the letters M-O-H-A-M-M-E-D were etched into the clouds. She asked me if Mohammed was in my Bible. I told her only true prophets of God were in the Bible, and Mohammed was not one of them. I opened my Bible to 2 Thessalonians 2:9–10 to shed light on what Rosa had experienced. I read, "The Anarchist's coming is all Satan's work. All his power and signs and miracles are fake, evil sleight of hand that plays so the gallery of those who hate the truth that could save them."

I looked at Rosa and said, "The sign in the clouds was a counterfeit, just as Mohammed was a false prophet, but God in his mercy has heard your cry and has sent me to tell you his good news." I shared the gospel message with Rosa and asked her if she wanted to make Jesus the Lord of her life and renounce Mohammed and his lie. With tears in her eyes, Rosa nodded yes, and that morning she was born again and translated out of the kingdom of darkness. I looked into Rosa's eyes and saw the light. She squeezed my hand and said, "Thank you."

As I was leaving Rosa began to cry, and I asked her what was wrong. She said, "My people in Iran do not know Jesus and are going to hell."

I smiled and replied, "No, you will share Jesus with your people and they will join you in his kingdom." At the time I had no idea Rosa had a daily radio program that she broadcasted to Iran and that God would use her to share the good news to this dark region of the earth.

The next day I made a visit at Rosa's business to make sure they were satisfied with my product. When I walked into the office, I noticed the atmosphere was markedly different—it was full of light, and the heavy oppression had lifted. The office had been cleaned and broken furniture replaced. Al came out, warmly greeted me, and then asked, "What did you do to my wife?" I smiled at him and he smiled back, and no words were necessary at that point. I have had many other experiences like this where people living in darkness are drawn to the Light and want to know what it is. I always have a choice when I am confronted with these situations—whether to follow the leading of the Holy Spirit or not. It is never about me or my convenience but about people whom Jesus died for, people he wants me to reach out to and invite into his kingdom. Jesus came to the earth as a humble servant. Following him requires humility, sacrifice, and selflessness as we are called to serve, no matter what we do in life.

As a servant I had to have the heart and compassion of Jesus for people. As a warrior I had to know my enemy, and this was the time I would face my giant of fear. Even though I was a highly trained police officer who never showed fear, I found myself bound by that spirit. The battle ground was no longer in the natural realm, so the carnal weapons I had relied upon in the past were utterly useless in the spiritual realm. The Holy Spirit began to train me to be aware of the presence of fear and to resist submitting to it. When I faced something fearful he would ask me, "What's that?" I knew he was referring to the fear I was feeling and I had to press through it.

One early summer morning, I was out riding my mountain bike through the canyons. The sun had not yet come up, and I was enjoying the stillness of this time of day. I rode through a ravine and had just crested a hill when I felt something rise up in me. I stopped just in time to avoid running into a diamond-back rattlesnake coiled in the middle of the trail. As I looked at the snake, I felt the fear overcoming me when I heard the Holy Spirit say, "Throw a rock at it." I thought, *There is no way I am going to agitate this snake and run the risk of being bitten in the middle of the desert.* The Holy Spirit again told me to throw a rock at it. I bent down, picked up a rock, and tossed it at the snake, hitting its tail. I was surprised when the snake did not move. I picked up another rock and hit it, and again, the snake remained motionless. The fear I was feeling left me, and I knew at that moment that it had no power to harm me. Psalm 91:13 says, "You'll walk unharmed among lions and snakes, and kick young lions and serpents from the path."

One night I awoke in a cold sweat, reeling with fear from a dream I just had. In the dream I was shutting my back door when a man with a distorted face, wearing a khaki work uniform rushed toward me. I quickly slammed the door and locked it. The man began to pick the lock as I moved to get my gun. The Holy Spirit then woke me from the dream and said, "The spirit of fear is at your door." I quickly got up, grabbed my gun, and went to the back door to check if it was still locked. Then

I went room to room, clearing my house of any intruders. As I headed back to bed the Holy Spirit said, "Wrong weapon!" I grabbed my Bible and looked up the word *weapon*. I read in 2 Corinthians 10:3–5, "The world is unprincipled. It's dog-eat-dog out there! The world doesn't fight fair. But we don't live or fight our battles that way—never have and never will. The tools of our trade aren't for marketing our manipulation, but they are for demolishing that entire massively corrupt culture. We use our powerful God-tools for smashing warped philosophies, tearing down barriers erected against the truth of God, fitting every loose thought and emotion and impulse into the structure of life shaped by Christ." "For though we live in the world, we do not wage war as the world does. The weapons we fight with are not the weapons of the world. On the contrary, they have divine power to demolish strongholds."

I had several visitations in the night, and in one particular situation the Holy Spirit told me to put on my armor. The Bible tells us in Ephesians 6:10–18, "God is strong, and he wants you strong. So take everything the Master has set out for you, well-made weapons of the best materials. And put them to use so you will be able to stand up to everything the devil throws your way. This is no afternoon athletic contest that we'll walk away from and forget about in a couple of hours. This is for keeps, a life-or-death fight to the finish against the devil and all his angels.

Be prepared. You're up against far more than you can handle on your own. Take all the help you can get, every weapon God has issued, so that when it's all over but the shouting you'll still be on your feet. Truth, righteousness, peace, faith, and salvation are more than words. Learn how to apply them. You'll need them throughout your life. God's Word is an indispensible weapon. In the same way, prayer is essential in this ongoing warfare. Pray hard and long. Pray for your brothers and sisters. Keep your eyes open. Keep each other's spirits up so that no one falls behind or drops out."

As a police officer, my armor consisted of a bulletproof vest, gun belt, baton, handcuffs, mace, and my gun, which were sufficient for battle in the natural world. When I left work I would take off my "armor," so I was not sure why the Holy Spirit wanted me to put on my armor before I went to sleep!

I found out the answer when I awoke at 12:40 a.m. in a sweat after fighting a dark spirit in my sleep. It choked me, punched and pushed me around as I tried to speak the name of Jesus. When I began to grow tired from wrestling with this demon I heard the Holy Spirit say, "Get up and take authority over it!" I sprang out of bed and said, "In the name of Jesus, I command you to leave!" The dark presence left, and I felt my skin crawling at the thought of that spirit touching me.

I had another visitation while sleeping and felt that gripping, disabling fear rise up and overtake me. I resisted and fought to get out of my dream. When I awoke I saw a dark figure standing in the doorway of my bedroom. The figure was in the form of a man and had wings behind him. I noticed he was wearing a priest's collar around his neck that appeared to glow in the dark. He told me he was there to give me my last rites before he killed me. He did not speak with words but with thoughts, and I replied, "The Lord rebuke you, Satan, depart from me!" He left, and the Holy Spirit said, "Satan has the power of suggestion, but you have the power of protection!" In the visitation Satan had masqueraded himself as an angel of light, a counterfeit high priest. First Corinthians 11:4 says, "Satan does it all the time, dressing up as a beautiful angel of light.

Ephesians 6:12 tells us, "For our struggle is not against flesh and blood, but against the rulers, against the authorities, against the powers of this dark world, and against the spiritual forces of evil in the heavenly realms" (NIV). It was all beginning to make sense to me. I now understood that the battle I had endured on the police department really was not about the men, but the spirits that were operating through them. When I made a commitment to follow Jesus, I was immediately inducted into a spiritual army and placed out on the front lines. Now I understood why there was such hatred toward me by these men in positions of authority on the police department.

I remember walking out of the civil service hearing during the appeal of my demotion on the police department when my brother Steve stopped me. He said, "You may not be a captain in man's police department, but you will be a general in God's army!" Steve had spoken prophetically and I discovered that when you are about to be promoted in God's kingdom, you can expect a demotion in man's kingdom. The Bible tells us not to be afraid or discouraged when man comes against us because the battle is not ours but God's. When the enemy attacked my authority in the natural realm, God established my authority in the spirit. When I was demoted two ranks, God gave me my first star as a general in his army.

During this time the Holy Spirit had instructed me to memorize Psalm 91 so I could speak it out of my mouth. He told me I must be able to speak the Word in the coming days. Hebrews 4:12 says, "God means what he says. What he says goes. His powerful Word is sharp as a surgeon's scalpel, cutting through everything, whether doubt or defense, laying us open to listen and obey. Nothing and no one is impervious to God's Word. We can't get away from it—no matter what." I would soon learn how powerful the word of God is when spoken from our mouth and the importance of obedience.

On December 24, 2006, I faced a battle for my life when I awoke at 3:00 a.m., unable to breathe. As I gasped for air, I hit the speed dial on my phone to call my friend Lisa. She answered the phone and, recognizing my voice, she had her husband,

Dave, call 911. A few minutes later the paramedics arrived at my home, and I was rushed to the hospital. As I lay in the back of the ambulance with the oxygen mask over my face, I began to pray Psalm 91. I now knew why God had told me to memorize the scripture. I struggled for each breath, and I expected an angel to appear at any moment to take me home. I again forgave everyone I could think of and let the Lord know I was ready to go when I dozed off.

I woke up in the emergency room as the medical team was working frantically to open my airway. After the CAT scan the doctor came in and told me he did not understand how I was able to breathe, because my airway had constricted to the size of a swizzle stick. He diagnosed me with acute epiglottis and informed me they were going to transport me to another hospital where there was a specialist on call. It was now early morning, and after being stabilized, I was lifted back into the ambulance for the trip into the city. Again I prayed Psalm 91 and fell asleep.

At the second hospital as the medics pushed the gurney down the hallway, my airway closed off again, and I began to gasp for air. I was quickly wheeled into the emergency room and doctors told the staff to prepare me for ICU. After many hours of tests and procedures, my two Christian sisters, Debbie and Lisa, arrived and prayed for me. I later learned the emergency room nurse was also a Christian and had been praying for me while she performed her nursing duties.

After my friends left and while waiting to go to ICU, I dozed off and immediately was transported in the spirit to heaven's gates. I watched a fully armored soldier, slumped over on his brown horse, enter the gates. As the horse slowly strode up the main street in heaven, I suddenly realized the soldier was me. The horse stopped, and I fell to the ground. I was lying on my back, unable to move, when suddenly a blinding light came into my face shield. I squinted my eyes to see who it was and was

Debra Gauthier

surprised to see Jesus with his wonderful warm smile. I could feel the depth of his love as I began to weep. He gently took off my helmet and wiped the tears from my eyes. I felt protected and comforted by his compassion.

Jesus lifted me into his arms after removing my armor and carried me to the river near the street. I thought he was going to lower me into the river, but he did not. Instead he carried me down the incline, holding me close against his chest as the water rose around us until we were fully submerged in the water. I thought I was going to drown, but suddenly I took a deep breath. The airway in my throat opened, and I felt life come back into me. I don't know how long we were under the water when Jesus began to walk back up the embankment of the river. He carried me to a row of trees, reached up, and pulled off one of the leaves and gently placed it in my mouth. As soon as the sweet grainy substance touched my tongue, it began to dissolve and I immediately felt strength come back into my body. I held onto Jesus and asked him if I could stay. He replied, "It's not time yet." He carried me back to my horse and helped me get dressed in my armor. He gently lifted me onto the horse and turned him toward the gate. With a smile he said, "Run your race; finish your course, fight the good fight of faith!"

When I came out of the vision, the ENT doctor ordered the nurse to prepare me for a procedure in which a scope is run down my throat. When the scope was in place, the doctor looked puzzled and said, "I don't see any evidence of acute epiglottis." Then another specialist came in and ordered another CAT scan, saying it was impossible that my condition would have reacted to the steroids and been resolved so quickly. The CAT scan confirmed that my airway was wide open and my throat was normal. The doctor told me he would admit me for the night for observation.

A few hours later I was moved upstairs to a private room, where I began to finally doze off. As I drifted into sleep, I saw myself inside a plastic bubble. It was translucent, and I could see the shape of a snake moving around the outside of the bubble. It kept pressing its tongue against the sides in an effort to strike me. I never felt any fear, but suddenly I sat up with a searing pain running from my IV into my arm. As I pressed the nurse's button, my throat again began to close off, and I couldn't breathe. I frantically continued to press the button, but no one came and panic began to set in.

As I tried to get out of bed, a nurse came running in and quickly assisted me. She told me she was walking past my door and something told her to come in even though she was not assigned to my wing. After being stabilized, I requested to be released because I knew the Holy Spirit was telling me to leave. The doctor refused to release me, so I signed a waiver and my friend came to pick me up. Psalm 91:14–16 says, "If you'll hold on to me for dear life," says God, "I'll get you out of any trouble. I'll give you the best of care if you'll only get to know and trust me. Call me and I'll answer, be at your side in bad times; I'll rescue you, and then throw you a party. I'll give you a long life, give you a long drink of salvation!"

A year after this incident, I was attending a Prophetic Conference in Portland, Oregon, when a man named Don asked me if he could share a word from the Lord. I had never met this man before, but I said yes. He said, "I saw you standing next to a white horse and then step and swing up into the saddle. The saddle was black leather with chrome designs on it…and the Lord would say to you that you are an heir to the Father and joint heir to the Son. What has been in the past will not be in the future. You will know the same power and authority that your brother Jesus has. The Holy Spirit will teach you, step by step, to walk in this new level of understanding, to the next new level of understanding. The Word will come forth out of your mouth with much authority and will not return void. The spoken Word will come out of your mouth and touch the one I will show you. It will come forth out of your mouth like a sword and will surprise the one you are speaking to, but it will not harm them. It will surgically accomplish that which I desire. Your friend and ally will be the Word of God. The name on the black saddle, written in silver, was Enforcer of Truth."

The apostle John describes the same rider and white horse in Revelation 19:11–13. "Then I saw Heaven open wide—and oh! a white horse and its Rider. The Rider, named Faithful and True, judges and makes war in pure righteousness. His eyes are a blaze of fire, on his head many crowns. He has a Name inscribed that's known only to himself. He is dressed in a robe soaked with blood, and he is addressed as 'Word of God.'"

I believe our journey on this Earth is training ground for reigning with Jesus in the millennial kingdom that will be established upon his return. Don had seen a picture of me in the spirit as part of Jesus's army. You might be asking how you can become a part of God's army. My answer to you is surrender! First, you surrender your life to Jesus, and then you follow him. It is not an easy road, but it is a rewarding one to know that one day we will stand before King Jesus and hear him say, "Well done, good and faithful servant."

The spirit of God's kingdom is faith, unlike the spirit of the world, which is fear. Hebrews 11:1 says, "The fundamental fact of existence is that this trust in God, this faith, is the firm foundation under everything that makes life worth living. It's our handle on what we can't see." I had a revelation of this verse in an unusual situation with my friend Debbie. While cutting my hair, she mistakenly cut my bangs way too short. It reminded of the time as a little girl when I got a hold of a pair of scissors and cut my bangs off the day I was having my school picture taken. I still have that picture of me with no bangs and a big smile! I was, however, not smiling much at this moment, and I could see this had upset Debbie, so I reached out and hugged her and told her not to worry.

That night Debbie said the Holy Spirit woke her up to pray, and she began pulling on her hair. Then she heard the Spirit say, "*Nothing is irreversible, and nothing is too difficult for me!*" The next morning I was getting ready for work and noticed that my bangs were longer; in fact, they had grown at least an inch while I slept!

Debbie put together a collage of pictures from my career as a police officer as a tribute to my life. She wrote the following words:

I am FREE to be a shining light in a
dark nation within the police department;
I am FREE to esteem others;
I am FREE to be in command,
to correct and discipline;
I am FREE to support my troops;
I am FREE to have true friends;
I am FREE to lay hands on the
sick and see them recover;
I am FREE to fight the good fight of faith;
I am FREE to praise my God;
I am FREE to run my race with
great joy and finally,
I am FREE to wait on the Lord and
in due season He will exalt me.
The curse has been reversed!
I am blessed of the Lord!
I am empowered to prosper!
I am the head and not the tail!
I am above only and not beneath!
I'm walking in favor!
I'm walking in the promise!
My body is whole in the name of JESUS!
I'm walking in divine health in
the name of JESUS!
GLORY TO GOD!
RESTORATION AND REWARD
are mine in the name of JESUS!

Once we have faced our giants and taken back the land in our own soul, we are ready to do what Jesus called his disciples to do in Mark 16:15–16 when He said, "Go into the world. Go everywhere and announce the Message of God's good news to one and all. Whoever believes and is baptized is saved; whoever refuses to believe is damned." Before we go it is important to have an encounter with Jesus so we can share his love with others.

I had such an encounter at a conference in Phoenix called "At His Feet." It was held during resurrection weekend, so it was very powerful. During worship I heard the Holy Spirit say, "Take off your shoes. You are standing on holy ground." As soon as I removed my shoes, I was overcome by the presence of a holy God, and I began to tremble and weep. When I opened my eyes, I saw in the spirit, Jesus standing across from me at arm's length. We were facing each other, and my eyes locked onto his fiery eyes filled with love and deep compassion. While he was staring at me, he reached his hand into his chest and pulled out his heart, which was pulsating causing beams of light to dance around the room. He smiled, and spoke with his eyes, "Your turn." I did what I saw him do and reached into my chest and pulled out my heart of flesh and held it out to him. He thrust his heart into my chest, and the rays of light came spilling out of me. I placed my heart into his chest. In John 17:20–23 Jesus prayed, "I'm praying not only for them but also for those who will believe in me because of them and their witness about me. The goal is for all of them to become one heart and mind—Just as you, Father, are in me and I in you, so they might be one heart and mind with us. Then the world might believe that you, in fact, sent me. The same glory you gave me, I gave them, so they'll be as unified and together as we are—I in them and you in me. Then they'll be mature in this oneness, and give the godless world evidence that you've sent me and loved them in the same way you've loved me."

With my new heart, I was ready for my next assignment. It came through a friend who gave me a business card of a chiropractic office. The business's logo was a New Age lotus symbol, and my first thought was, *There is no way I am going there.* I heard the Holy Spirit say, "Go, I am sending you!"

My response was, "This is a New Age office. Shouldn't I be concerned about transference of spirits?" The Holy Spirit reminded me that "greater is he who is in me than he who is in the world." So I went.

I made an appointment and immediately upon entering the chiropractic office, I noticed the Buddha statue and all the other Hindu occult symbols. The receptionist smiled at me, and I said to her, "I see you are spiritual." She nodded and warmly welcomed me. As I sat in the lobby, one of the masseuses walked by. I motioned toward her and said, "I see you are a warrior!" Her name was Becky and she had tattoos, piercings, and all the other markings of the god of this world.

She smiled and replied, "How did you know that?"

"I just knew." My instructions from the Holy Spirit were to bring the light into the darkness and to be His witness without words. I thought, *How am I going to be a witness without my mouth?*

When I walked into the treatment room, I saw several patients sitting against the wall and the two female chiropractors in the middle of the room working on patients. I thought, this is an interesting set-up. Everyone stopped talking when I came into the room. As I sat waiting for my turn, I was reminded of John 3:16–17, which says, "This is how much God loved the world: He gave his Son, his one and only Son. And this is why: so that no one need be destroyed; by believing in him, anyone can have a whole and lasting life. God didn't go to all the trouble of sending his Son merely to point an accusing finger, telling the world how bad it was. He came to help, to put the world right again."

Debra Gauthier

Becky, at the far end of the room, began telling the doctors about a patient she had recently worked on who began to sing gospel songs to her during the massage session. She looked over at me and smiled, and I said nothing. At my next visit, Becky was telling the doctors about her weekend. She had gone downtown drinking with her friends and had been intrigued by a woman with a megaphone and sign that said, "Repent, Jesus is coming soon!" Becky told the doctors she was impressed that the woman was so passionate about her message in spite of the crowd's ridicule.

I discerned a mocking religious spirit in this office, and the Holy Spirit told me to take authority over it. I knew I was on assignment, so I entered into intercession and fought the good fight in the spirit. Week after week I went to the office to get an adjustment. The doctor made a comment one day that I was fighting her manipulations. I admitted to her that it was true. This woman was in deep darkness and would not even make eye contact with me. When I came into the room, the conversation always shifted to God. I knew they were trying to engage me in discussion and I would have loved to verbally spar with them, but I remained obedient to the Holy Spirit and said nothing.

Finally a door opened when Becky said, "I want to know about the warrior's journey." She began to share about her father, a Christian man who, when she was just a little girl, went into the woods by their house and shot himself. My heart was moved with compassion. I felt her pain when she said, "I'm afraid I will turn my warrior spirit against myself." I reached out with Jesus's heart of compassion and embraced this broken woman when to my surprise I heard the Holy Spirit say, "This is a demonstration of my power!"

On my last visit to the chiropractor, Becky was scheduled to work on me. While alone in her room she asked me, "Do you have to be a Christian to be a warrior?"

"How do you mean?"

"Well," she said, "Christians are a bunch of hypocrites and I want no part of that." She paused and then added, "You're a Christian, aren't you?"

"What is your definition of a Christian?" I asked her.

She gave me her religious definition of a Christian, and I said, "Based on your definition, no!"

Surprised by my reply she said, "I guess I shouldn't have assumed!"

I told her many people call themselves Christians but I was a follower of Jesus and there was a difference. She asked me what the difference was and I said, "Surrender." I looked into the eyes of an abandoned little girl and said, "Jesus has sent me to you, and he is calling you into his kingdom. Will you surrender?"

She hesitated, and I said, "The journey of a warrior is a place of surrender," and I shared my testimony. Becky began to cry as I shared how Jesus had reached out his hand to me and I had to make a decision to take his hand and follow him. As I reached out my hand to Becky, I said, "Jesus, the Warrior King, is inviting you to come and follow him."

Becky, choking back the tears, grabbed my hand in desperation and held it tight as she bowed her knee.

I was beginning to understand what the apostle Paul meant in 1 Corinthians 2:1–4:

> You'll remember, friends, that when I first came to you to let you in on God's master stroke, I didn't try to impress you with polished speeches and the latest philosophy. I deliberately kept it plain and simple: first Jesus and who he is; then Jesus and what he did—Jesus crucified.
> I was unsure of how to go about this, and felt totally inadequate—I was scared to death, if you want the truth of it—and so nothing I said

Debra Gauthier

could have impressed you or anyone else. But the Message came through anyway. God's Spirit and God's power did it, which made it clear that your life of faith is a response to God's power, not to some fancy mental or emotional footwork by me or anyone else.

The world is no longer moved by Christians who talk the talk but do not walk the walk. Perhaps that is why I believe the Holy Spirit is raising up a company of warriors in this hour that will go into the enemy's camp and confront the powers of darkness and demonstrate the power of Jesus's love.

A few days after Becky had encountered the power of Jesus's love, I received a text from her that said, "The other day gave me a lot to think about. It's a lot right now ..."

I continued to pray for her until the Holy Spirit said, "Your assignment is over!" The Lord has called me to very dark places and has impressed upon me the importance of timing when in these places. The Holy Spirit used the movie *The Matrix* to teach me how to move in and out of this realm.

A week later I was getting ready to go to bed when I saw flashes of light in my right eye. It looked like the eclipse of the sun where I could see these flashes on the edge of the inside of my eye. I went to sleep and woke up with the same sensations and flashes in my right eye. I called my eye doctor and he told me to meet him at his office even though it was Saturday and they were closed. My doctor examined me and found a tear in the retina. He immediately sent me to a specialist. I met with Dr. Lou, who confirmed that I had a tear on the retina of my right eye. He then explained how the eye has a matrix behind it that acts as a lattice to hold the collagen in place. The collagen is a gel that was useful during primitive times to protect the eye from collapsing when struck. He told me that when the matrix collapses, the collagen no longer has a structure to adhere to, and it floats around in this area. This is why I was seeing "floaters" in my eye, which were obstructing my vision. The doctor said, "Your matrix has collapsed and caused a tear in the retina." I am thinking, *Did he just say what I think he said?* The Holy Spirit began to reveal to me that this matrix is the access point or gateway the enemy uses to enter our mind. Since mine had collapsed, the enemy would no longer have an access point to enter into the dream realm. I recalled in the movie that when the matrix fell, the people were freed and the machines were no longer able to attack them.

The Spirit of God was showing me that the matrix represents the world, which is the devil's territory. When entering the world, we need to stay focused on our assignment, follow orders and strategies of the Holy Spirit, complete the assignment, and get out when it's over. Timing is critical in this realm; to stay in the matrix longer makes us vulnerable and susceptible to the enemy's attack. It was all beginning to make sense to me, and I realized that most people, like those in the movie, are oblivious to this reality.

Dr. Lou said he needed to perform emergency laser surgery to prevent a detachment of the retina, which would result in blindness. He put numbing drops in my eye and told me to keep my eyes closed until they brought me back into the surgery room. As I sat in an optical chair, the lights dimmed, I could not see with my natural eyes, yet my spiritual eyes were wide open. That's when I saw Jesus walk into the room. He came up to me, leaned over, and kissed my right eyelid, my left eyelid, and my forehead. He smiled, turned, and walked out. After several minutes the technician came in and escorted me back to the surgery room.

As I was lying on the table, still unable to see in the natural, I could clearly see in the spirit and noticed a large angel beside me covering me with his wing. When the doctor approached, the

Debra Gauthier

angel lifted his wing and stood at the foot of the table watching. Psalm 91:11 says, "He ordered his angels to guard you where you go." The procedure was excruciatingly painful as the laser welded the tissue together. It felt like that sharp stabbing pain you feel when you eat something cold too quickly. That was the intensity of the pain I had to endure for fifteen minutes. Now I knew why the angel was standing there. So I could be still, knowing that the angel was protecting me. As I drove home with one good eye, I asked the Holy Spirit what that was all about. I heard Him say, "You asked about the matrix and how the enemy gains accesses to you as you sleep, and I have just revealed the answer."

"Wasn't there an easier way to reveal that to me?" I asked.

"No pain, no gain!" He said.

I laughed and then began to sing, "There's been an explosion in my eye; now I can see and now I can fly like the eagle." I read once how an eagle knows when a storm is approaching long before it breaks. The eagle will fly to a high spot and wait for the winds to come. When the storm hits, it sets its wings so that the wind will pick it up and lift it above the storm. While the storm rages below, the eagle is soaring above it. The eagle doesn't escape the storm. It simply uses the storm to lift it higher. It rises on the winds that bring the storm. This is how we live in the kingdom. God enables us to ride the winds of the storms that bring sickness, tragedy, failure, and disappointment in our lives to drive us higher in the spirit. Like the eagle we are designed to soar above the storm. What an adventure!

"You Want Me to Do What, God?"

Do you see what this means—all these pioneers who blazed the way, all these veterans cheering us on? It means we'd better get on with it. Strip down, start running—and never quit?

Hebrews 12:1

The wilderness is meant to break us of our self-sufficiency so we can learn to trust God. When that work was completed and I was a mess, I heard the Holy Spirit say, "Arise, mighty woman of valor!" I thought, *Not again, God!* It was the spring of 2002, one year after I had left the police department. This morning I walked out to my driveway and picked up a newspaper. I thought it was strange because I did not subscribe to the paper. I opened it to the front page, and in bold print it announced the filing for the upcoming sheriff's race. I got this funny feeling that God wanted me to run for sheriff so an angel must have brought the paper. I quickly dismissed it; after all, who would vote for someone who had been terminated from the police department!

Then I remembered the dream I had had while I was going through my trial on the department. In my dream I saw myself as a little girl running up to the throne of God. I yelled with excitement, "Daddy, Daddy, look what I've got," as I jumped up into the heavenly Father's lap. He looked and I showed him my captain's bars. He smiled and said, "I've got something for you." My eyes got big when I saw him clutching something in his hand. I begged him to let me see what was in his hand, and when he opened it, I saw five shiny stars. He then asked me if

I wanted the stars or the bars. I quickly responded, "The stars, because you made them!" I presumed that not only was I going to be reinstated as a captain, but I would later become the sheriff. However, I was demoted, losing my career, my reputation, and two-thirds of my retirement. Plus my insurance trust was cancelled, leaving me without medical benefits.

At church later that week, the preacher stopped his service and said, "Whatever the Lord told you to do…do it!" Again, I dismissed it as just a coincidence; surely he was not talking to me. Finally my good friend Debbie called. She told me she was interceding for me and the Lord showed her that I was to run for sheriff. I was about to fulfill 1 Corinthians 1:27–28, which says, "Isn't it obvious that God deliberately chose men and women that the culture overlooks and exploits and abuses, chose these 'nobodies' to expose the hallow pretensions off the 'somebodies'"?

On May 20, 2002, at 2:15 p.m. I reluctantly arrived at the election department and parked in a space close to the front door. I walked in and there was no line, so I quickly completed the paperwork to file for the public office of Clark County Sheriff. I truly looked like a fool for Jesus. Before I could complete the process I needed to provide information on a campaign headquarters. The Holy Spirit told me to call my friend Betty. When I told her I was filing for office, she asked if I needed a campaign headquarters. She told me she would gladly let me use her business office and she would set up additional phone lines.

When I walked back into the election department to finish the paperwork, it was now crowded with candidates filing at the end of the last day. I told the clerk that I now had a campaign headquarters and a telephone number. I was delayed in the office long enough for the newspaper reporter to arrive. He asked me if he could take an action shot of my filing for sheriff, and that photo hit the newspaper the very next day. I would be running against ten men, several of whom had been instrumental in my

Debra Gauthier

downfall at the police department. As I left the election department, a woman approached me, introducing herself as the president of the National Organization of Women. She invited me to speak at the "Meet the Candidate" night in June. I accepted her invitation and knew the race had begun.

Several days after filing for office, the Lord spoke these words to me:

> Do not look to man for acceptance; I love you and accept you. To whom much is given, much is expected. I have given you much, dear one. Be wise as a serpent and harmless as a dove. I will contend with those who contend with you. Do not fear. I *am* with you. I will fill you as you empty yourself. I will show you the way to walk. Stay close to me. There is no place for fear or doubt. It is not you but my anointing that is going forth. Do not underestimate the power of the anointing. Your flesh cannot contain it; you must yield and flow with my Spirit.
>
> I know this is hard. My grace is sufficient in your weakness. Remember, when you are weak, then you are strong. I am teaching you to stand in the anointing; to stand you must have a pure heart. My word must become your words. There is power in my word. You have been called to this city for this time. Run the sheriff's race in faith; every step of obedience will bring you closer to your destiny. I *am* here, do not fear! Psalm 91 is for your protection; speak it often. The situation at your church is a distraction from the enemy, who is trying to steal your anointing.
>
> Stand firm, stay focused, and maintain your peace. Do not be moved by any of it; remember to keep your heart pure. You grow through adversity; you cannot have a victory without a battle.

Remember what I told you about your hearing becoming supernatural. This is why the enemy has attacked you in your ears. You have broken through the barrier and your hearing will be sensitive to my Spirit. This has all been a test and is preparation for where you are going. Be anxious for nothing, but in all things give praise and thanks to me.

In an effort to get the campaign started right, I met with several campaign managers, but with no funds to pay them, those doors quickly closed. I was looking for assistance in the natural realm, but the Lord knew I would need assistance in the spirit, so he called five prayer warriors to intercede during my campaign. The Lord assigned a man named Ed to be my armor bearer. I met Ed and his wife, Barbara, at a church event. As I sat across from them, Ed, who was blind in one eye, said, "The Lord has given you the ability to see your enemies." Ed had come to Las Vegas from back East, not knowing what God had for him to do. The Lord revealed to Ed that he would be my armor bearer and battle for me in the spirit.

When I announced my candidacy to my home church, the pastor started singing, "Who shot the sheriff?" I did not find that humorous, and I knew whose side this man was on. The Lord used that incident to lead me out of the big, white, prosperous church out into the community to the smaller minority churches where I would find my support. It made no sense, since the one thing I lacked was resources and the smaller churches could not support me in that way. I ran a grassroots campaign, relying on a small group of volunteers. I was amazed that people would come up to me when I was on the campaign trail and tell me they had seen my signs. I found that odd and funny because I didn't have any signs. It was a miracle that I was even in this race, and I knew God was going to get all the glory.

The first major event I participated in was a public debate where I would sit beside two men who had played active roles in my ruin. I struggled with fear, and I knew the Lord was not pleased when he said, "Who are these men? Are they greater than me?" Nahum 1:2 says, "God is serious business. He won't be trifled with. He avenges his foes. He stands up against his enemies, fierce and raging." The Holy Spirit encouraged me with the following words; his words became life to me during this campaign.

> Be still and know that I *am* God. Go, the way has been prepared, walk in the anointing. Face your giants in the land that I *am* giving you. Do not be dismayed or discouraged, for I *am* with you. Remember, it is not what you see in the natural, but what you see in the spirit that is important. You are my chosen one. Never doubt, only shout! For your victory awaits you on the hill. Now, about this race; run it in faith. I have given you favor everywhere you go. Just show up, and I will do the rest. It will be an upset in the enemy's camp.

Although I didn't have money, I did have favor, and many doors opened for me to speak. I would open each speech by stating that I was qualified to be the sheriff with twenty-one years as a police officer obtaining the rank of lieutenant, with a master's degree in public administration and, most importantly, that Jesus Christ was my Lord and Savior, and he had called me to this race. I'll never forget the looks I got, ranging from shock to excitement. Never once was I challenged for mentioning the name of Jesus, whether I was in a secular business meeting or speaking to the National Organization of Women.

In the months leading up to the election, I made the rounds with my staff, appearing in parades, walking the district on foot meeting with business owners, and knocking on residents' doors asking for their vote. I spoke at just about every civic and community organization in town in an effort to reach the voters and gain their support. I stood on a platform of integrity and used my termination from the police department as a forum for positive change. I ran the sheriff's race like we were going to win. I knew nothing was impossible with God, and I stood on Philippians 3:13–14, which says, "Friends, don't get me wrong: By no means do I count myself an expert in all of this, but I've got my eye on the goal, where God is beckoning us onward—to Jesus. I'm off and running, and I'm not turning back." On September 3, 2002, my team met at campaign headquarters as we watched the votes come in for the primary election. The top two candidates would go on to the general election in November. When the numbers were tallied, I came in fourth place. Although we were disappointed, I knew in the spiritual realm it was a victory and God was pleased with his servants. Isaiah 9:2: "The people who walked in darkness have seen a great light. For those who lived in a land of deep shadows—light! sunbursts of light!" was fulfilled. I will not know how many people were impacted for the kingdom until I get on the other side of the glory.

So why would God have me run in a race that I could not possibly win? Perhaps the race was to bring his light into the darkness and prepare the fields for harvest. It wasn't about me winning; it was about what Jesus has already won. It reminded me of the vision I had where I saw a passenger train filled with people speeding across a valley. The train was hell bound, and I saw myself riding on a horse with a scroll in my hand racing to get in front of the train. Is that what had happened in the spirit? Maybe the people who were touched by my campaign were on that train and something in their hearts was ignited and hope released. I do not understand it all, and I can't explain many of the things that happened. But I do know that Jesus is long suffering and he wants no one to perish.

I left the campaign trail and hit the mountain bike trail to gain some perspective. One day as I rode along a narrow path, a strange-looking lizard with tall legs leaped out in front of my front tire. In all my years living in the desert, I had never seen any reptile like this before. It even acted strange, and instead of doing what most lizards do when they cross your path and get out of the way, this one ran out on the trail in front of me. I watched in amazement as I heard the Spirit say, "You've got the devil on the run!" I realized then that what had happened in the spiritual realm during the sheriff's race was much different than what I saw in the natural realm; what looked like defeat was really victory!

As I look back over the last twelve years, it has been an amazing journey walking with the King of kings. Who would have known that Jesus would bring a frightened little girl from desperation into his glorious kingdom on the hill of restoration? Only God could orchestrate such events and turn a tragedy into a triumph. I will not see the complete picture and the beautiful tapestry of my life until I cross over into glory.

Although much of this journey has been difficult and the hardships have been overwhelmingly painful, I am truly amazed at how God takes our mess and makes it our message, never wasting any trial that we face. I may not understand the reason for all of it, but I have grown to trust the Lord of all of it and to rely on Holy Spirit's help through the tough places. In my first encounter with Jesus, he told me that no man would get the glory for what he was going to do in my life. I am beginning to understand what he meant by that as I have come to the same place where the apostle Paul found himself in Philippians 3:8–10. "Yes, all the things I once thought were so important are gone from my life. Compared to the high privilege of knowing

Christ Jesus as my Master, firsthand, everything I once thought I had going for me is insignificant—dog dung. I've dumped it all in the trash so that I could embrace Christ and be embraced by him. I didn't want some petty, inferior brand of righteousness that comes from keeping a list of rules when I could get the robust kind that comes from trusting Christ—God's righteousness. I gave up all that inferior stuff so that I could know Christ personally, experience his resurrection power, be a partner in his suffering, and go all the way with him to death itself."

There is something to be said about going through adversity that brings us closer to the One who suffered a violent death on our behalf. As we share in the sufferings of Jesus, we grow more and more in his likeness until there is nothing left but him. It is then that we can humbly offer ourselves as living sacrifices and share with others our stories for his glory. I pray that you have been touched by my story and have identified with your need for a Savior. Go ahead and receive his gift of living water. It's absolutely free. See you in Heaven!